COCKTAILS
and SHOTS
for PARTY'S
2014

Lundeen,
Richard, 1963
[i. Alcoholic
Beverages]

Printed in the
United States
of America

ISBN-13: 978-
1478390909:

Richard
Lundeen

An alphabetized listing of
popular party drinks and
shots for any occasion

Dedicated to --

The Shadow Boyz of Rush Street

COCKTAILS and SHOTS for PARTY'S

Richard Lundeen

History of Cocktails

The history of mixed drinks dates to the 1800s. Back then, mixed drinks were little more than a kind of style of alcohol such as punch or fizz. What separated the mixed drink from other spirits was the combination of a base alcohol with water, bitters and often something sweet. Although the average cocktail today is imbibed in a loud nightclub or bar, the very first mixed drinks were designed as an energy booster to consume in the morning.

The first genuinely significant mixed drink was the Sazerac, which began showing around New Orleans in the 1860s. The Sazerac was a concoction devised with cognac and absinthe. Cognac was a natural choice for the world's first popular cocktail because it was inside so many homes and bars at the time. The death knell of cognac as the prime base spirit for mixed drinks had to do with a parasitic contamination in the vines of France. Afterward, rye became the primary base.

Most mixed drinks are today identified as cocktails, and the origin of the word cocktail may never be known for certain. One theory posits that cock was the word for the spigot from which alcohol was poured and tail was a term used to describe the very last remnants of the tank. A much better story has to do with a tavern owner named Betsy Flanagan who during the Revolutionary War would use the tail feather of a rooster as a garnish. Thus the term cock-tail.

Some mixed drinks require ice. The importance of adding ice to a mixed drink has more to do with it than merely cooling the alcohol. Ice is used in a mixed drink more for the purpose of adding water than keeping it cold. How much ice or even the type of ice used, such as cubed or crushed, is an important element in creating a new mixed drink or making an existing drink. The larger the ice the longer it takes to dissolve, therefore the larger the glass the more likely it will be to have an abundance of ice. Too much ice in a smaller glass will water down the alcohol to the point when it becomes almost pointless to consume.

Every James Bond knows he likes his martini shaken and not stirred. The reason that Mr. Bond probably prefers that particular mixed drink shaken rather than stirred is due to the physics of chilling a drink. Shaking a mixed drink with ice has the effect of making it colder than even vigorous stirring, not to mention the fact that stirring will usually leave unwanted chips of ice. The only time it is recommended to stir rather than shake a mixed drink, in fact, is if the mixed drink is made entirely of alcohol.

Misconceptions

Some people, including bartenders, believe that certain drinks must be served in specific types of glasses. For instance, the mixed drink cocktail known as the martini actually gave rise to a specific shape of glass known as the martini glass. While a martini probably won't taste as good in any other kind of glass purely for psychological reasons, serving a recognized mixed drink in a different and unexpected glass won't hurt the taste and may even create more interest in it. The shape of the glass that mixed drinks are traditionally served in usually has a history based upon necessity at the moment rather than any integral connection between style and taste.

One of the most recognizable effects of a mixed drink is the garnish. The garnish can be anything from an olive in a martini to a carrot in a bloody Mary. Any fresh garnishes should be cut as close to serving time as possible; if you intend to cut them ahead of time, keep them in the refrigerator overnight. Tradition dictates that garnishes be served in odd numbers. In other words, most drinks will contain one or three olives or onions rather than two.

Party Time

Part of being a great host for a party is being able to supply fun and interesting drinks for your visitors. Being a good bartender is actually easier than you think. Once you have a few key ingredients and the proper bartending tools, you will be mixing drinks that will have your guests begging you to tell them how you made it.

In order to be able to mix drinks at home, you are going to need a few basic pieces of equipment. These pieces of equipment are pretty affordable and will make your life much easier when you go to make your drinks.

Cocktail Shaker
Cocktail Strainer
Bar Mat
Shot Glasses
Collins Glasses
High Ball Glasses

A Cocktail Shaker is used for mixing up ingredients on ice, and likewise, the strainer is used to remove the liquid from the cocktail shaker while preventing pulp or thicker ingredients from entering your glass.

A bar mat is nice to have, because you place your shot glasses open side down on the mat after you pour drinks in order to prevent your counter top from getting extremely messy.

Shot glasses are used both for measuring ingredients when mixing a drink as well as for when your guests would like to do a shooter.

A Collins glass is a taller glass used for serving larger drinks and a high ball glass is a shorter glass typically used when serving smaller drinks such as a high ball.

On top of having all the equipment necessary to mix drinks, there are a handful of basic ingredients you should probably keep around the house to mix drinks.

These ingredients include:
 Sodas: Coke, 7up, tonic water, soda water, red bull
 Mixes: Sweet n Sour, Grenadine, Lime Cordial, Simple Syrup
 Garnishes: Lemon and lime wedges, Celery, Olives, Maraschino cherries
 Rimmers - There are a ton of different flavored rimmers for different drinks, buy them as needed
 Ice

Stocking Your Bar

For a basic bar the following are necessary:

Vodka	White wine
Bourbon whiskey	Beer
Bacardi rum	Angostura (4 oz size)
Gin	Bar syrup
Scotch	Mild Bloody Mary premix
Tequila	Sweet-sour premix
Southern Comfort	olives
Kahlua	whole stem cherries
Bailey's Irish Cream	Grenadine
Vermouth (small bottle)	Tomato juice
Triple Sec (small bottle)	Orange juice
Amaretto	fresh lemon/limes
Brandy or cognac	Margarita salt
Club soda	Ginger ale
7 – up	Squirt
Cola	ice-cubes

Popular Mixed Drinks

Party drinks are a great way to turn any party into lots of fun. Fruity cocktails and tropical drinks are sure to fit in perfectly with fun music and flashing lights. Some of the most popular and must have party drinks include Sex on the Beach, Shirley Temple, Orgasm, Alabama Slammer, Manhattan, Tequila Sunrise, Black Russian, Kamikaze, Pina Colada, Martini, Cosmopolitan, Screwdriver, Mojito, Apple Martini, Madouri Sour, Daiquiri, Harvey Wallbanger, and Irish Coffee. These drinks include vodka, rum, whiskey, and tequila, and usually take a knowledgeable bartender to prepare. It is best to hire a service to prepare the drinks so the host can relax and mingle with the crowd. It is important to keep in mind that mixed drinks often include more than one type of alcohol within one glass, and hence, have a tendency to intoxicate drinkers much more quickly than they are used to or anticipated. Different kinds of juices such as cranberry, orange, and pineapple are also a must have for any party. They are either usually mixed in with the alcohol or are used as chasers for shots. Don't forget the salt and lemon because these are often involved with taking shots as well. Jello shots are also a very popular concoction at parties. They are made from gelatin mixed with alcohol and chilled in the refrigerator until solid or wiggly. They are usually prepared in small, shallow, disposable containers that make swallowing the portions of Jello easy and fun.

Planning A Party

Invitations. It is best to invite by written invitation. Let the guest RSVP only with regrets. It is not in the best taste to invite more than two weeks before a party. This does not allow a graceful way for the guest to decline.

A written invitation also provides a ready refresher as to the time and date and does away with uncertainty. It also shows effort and thought on your part. It will provide you with an opportunity to scan your list to make certain that people who will be uncomfortable with each other are excluded, such as an ex-girl friend or ex spouse.

Take a few moments to determine traffic patterns in your home. It may be a good idea to set the bar up in one area and the food in another. People tend to congregate at these places and you thus avoid crowding.

What is the most comfortable pattern for your home? Where will coats be stored? How will seating be arranged? It may be wise to have food in two or three areas. Some thought on your part prior to the party can be extremely useful.

Is your party going to have a theme drink such as Pina Coladas, Margaritas or Bloody Marys? You should decide that prior the party. If it is a large party, you should plan only 2 mixed drinks. These should be served by the pitcher. The remaining mixed drinks should be simple drinks with water or on the rocks. A guest is rude if he requests a difficult mixed drink at a large gathering unless you have a professional bartender.

If possible, take note of the liquor and drinks consumed by the same people at a previous party. This information will be useful as to the amount and types of liquor and mixes you will need.

DECIDING ON HOW MUCH LIQUOR TO BUY

An important part of your party will be deciding on how much liquor to purchase.

Determine your total number of guests. If there is no RSVP, take the number of people that you invited and multiply it by .80 (80%). As a general rule, 20% of the people invited do not show up to a party. This gives you a good standard on which to base your calculations.

Now, consider the length of your party. In most cases, your guests will drink 2 drinks during the first hour and one per hour afterward. If you have a heavy-drinking crowd, you may want to up that number to a flat 2 per hour.

So, if 100 people are invited to a 4 hour party, you should need drinks for 80. 160 drinks for the first hour and 80 each hour afterward. That is a total of 400 drinks. If you purchase cans or bottles, the math is easy from there. If you are purchasing mixed drinks, consider a drink to be 8 ounces and do your math from there.

Martinis

Fifteen of the most popular Martini Recipes, from the classic dry martini to the new "dessert" martinis like cherry, vanilla and chocolate martinis. Martini-making tips, too.

Mojitos

All Mojito recipes feature rum, lime, and mint leaves. Some feel that the original, Classic Mojito Recipe, with just a little sugar and soda water added, is still the best.

But for those that feel Mojitos benefit from spiced rum, a splash of juice or a bit of passion fruit, raspberry, or vanilla, we have More (and Better) Mojito Recipes.

Wine and Champagne

For a drink that is both rich and refreshing try one of the Red Wine Sangria recipes, prepared with brandy or champagne, and fruit, and left to meld in the refrigerator for a time. Just right for a barbecue.

Special occasion Champagne Cocktail recipes for many or a single drink.

Margaritas

Like parking in the driveway and driving in the parkway, blended margaritas are stirred, not prepared in the blender. Find recipes for both frozen and blended Margaritas, including Avocado and Strawberry Margaritas.

Brunch Drinks

What drinks to serve with brunch? Try these time-honored Classic Brunch Drinks like Bellini, Ramos Fizz, Brunch Punch and Mimosa. Or serve true Irish coffee, an elegant after-dinner or brunch selection.

Blender Drinks

Our Blender Drink recipes include Strawberry Mimosa, Peach Delight, Mint Daiquiri, and Mississippi Mud.

(And let's not forget to include here the original 'frozen concoction that helps us hang on'-- Margaritas, above.)

The fundamentals of cocktails include:

Whiskey Cocktail Recipes

Whiskey cocktails tend to be dark and the varieties of whiskey lend their distinct flavors to the mixers they are combined with resulting in a wide range of tastes.

Vodka Cocktail Recipes

Vodka is the best spirit to keep around at all times and it is the most popular base spirit for cocktails. With an only a few mixers and liqueurs you can make a variety of cocktails, each with their own distinct taste.

It is a clear liquor manufactured from ethyl alcohol. It lacks color, and normally has very little taste or aroma.

Vodka is the base ingredient for many cocktails, mixed drinks, and alcoholic products today.

It is said to have been originally created from potatoes in Russia for medicinal purposes. Nowadays, Vodka is distilled from barley, wheat or rye.

Adulterated vodkas are now a popular alternative to the original. These will normally contain a mixture of sweeteners, flavorings, colorings and fruit juices. Most flavored vodka contains 30-35% alcohol, whereas clear vodka is normally 40%, with a few brands offering a 50% product on top.

Tequila Cocktail Recipes

Tequila is often used as a shooter but does also appear in some great cocktails like a Tequila Sunrise, Brave Bull and, of course, Margaritas.

Rum Cocktail Recipes

Rum is used for a variety of styles of cocktails including many of the tropical drinks

Gin Cocktail Recipes

Gin adds a light flavoring to many favorite cocktails. Some of the great recipes of all time are made with gin, including the popular Martini and many of its variations.

Brandy Cocktail Recipes

The unique fruity flavoring of brandy makes a great cocktail base

DRINK IDEAS FOR SPECIAL TIMES OF THE YEAR

HALLOWEEN

One of the great aspects about Halloween cocktails is that you can have a lot of fun with the presentation. This is the occasion in which you can think of your cocktail garnishes just as you would your costume and there is virtually no limit to where your imagination can take you. Below are a few simple suggestions to get you started in creating the creepiest of adornments for your drinks.

Take your pumpkin carving skills to a smaller medium by carving your garnish. This is a neat little trick that can go with almost any cocktail. All you need is a knife or channel knife, a little patience, and some fruit to practice with. The orange is a perfect candidate because of the orange color and thick skin. The trick is to carve out the orange peel, leaving a thin layer of the white pith visible. The second trick is to carefully peel the circle you cut from the fruit. Like I said, a little patience and practice and you have a great garnish.

Try this technique with other citrus fruit as well, or you can do the same with hot pepper garnishes, cutting through the entire skin. Another great addition to the orange face is to burn it as you would any burnt orange peel.

SLIME DRINKS

We're not really talking about "slime" here, but more of a swampy sludge look that can be added to your drinks. This technique works best with drinks that include egg like the Bayou Slime pictured because of the foam that is created when shaking and straining these drinks. The thick, white film that floats atop egg drinks is the ideal palate and any complimentary herb (in this case, mint) can be torn and scattered on top to complete the garnish. If an appropriate addition to the drink, add grated nutmeg or cinnamon for the look of dirt as well.

Capping a drink with a Pumpkin Top

This is a clever and easy garnish that can be used in a multitude of drinks, especially those with a concentration of orange juice. By having the orange colored drink as a base and serving a it in a short, round glass the full effect of the pumpkin can be achieved.

Constructing this garnish is simple: Cut an orange wheel and a small lime peel. Twist the lime and poke it into the middle of the orange. This faux pumpkin cap will float on your drink and adding a straw to one side of the orange makes the cocktail below easy to drink.

14

Drinks with Eyeballs

The eyeball is a creepy organ and there is no time better than Halloween to bring them out. There are many ways to construct eyeballs to use for garnishes and which you choose is going to depend a lot on the style of drink you are serving.

One of my favorite eyeballs is in the picture and goes with the Mad Eye Martini, though it can compliment any number of light flavored drinks. This one is made with a lychee, a blueberry, and fruit preserves, which create the veins. It is a great concept and the lychee is the perfect candidate for the casing because of its texture and membrane-like feel.

Another eyeball you might try for savory drinks involves a radish and an olive. The idea is part of this Vampire Juice drink. If the radish isn't going to fit your drink, but an olive will, you may want to think about stuffing the olive alone to simulate an eyeball. A little pimento (veins) can be stuffed in either black or green olives, and maybe you want to add a larger stuffing of capers, garlic, or jalapenos on the inside of that to act as the iris.

So the effect of your eyeball creations is not lost, don't drown them in the drink but skewer the eyes and rest it on top of the glass.

Drinks with Bloody Rims

Drinks that call for a sugar rim or that could be enhanced with one can be transformed into a slightly creepier version for Halloween. This can be created by simply using red or black sugar.

There are two options for colored sugar. You can usually find it in the baking section of the grocery store. It is typically used for decorating sweets but makes a colorful rimming option well. The alternative is to add food coloring to white sugar to make any color you want. For Halloween, I prefer the latter because the liquid turns the sugar into more of a gooey substance that sticks easily to the glass, though does also clump more.

Also, try running the rim through grenadine for a red base before the sugar for a more dynamic effect.

Drinks with Spider Webbing

I will admit, this is probably the most difficult garnish to pull off, but if you can get the technique down your drinks will be stellar. There are two ways to create the look of spider webs inside a glass. The more interesting and far trickier is demonstrated in the Spider's Kiss and involves drawing the web with chocolate syrup. The key here is to work fast and freeze the glass immediately to avoid too many runs in your syrup. Then again, dripping chocolate can be an interesting effect as well.

The other technique is seen in one of mixologist Victoria D'Amato-Moran's other Midori cocktails. In the Green Ghoul she uses black licorice strips placed along the sides and these are held in place by a generous pile of ice cubes.

Illumination for Drinks

Here is another very simple, yet effective, "garnish." Essentially, you're just adding a glow stick to your drinks. The dual advantage here is that you get a cool looking drink and a stir stick. An alternative to this is to wrap a glowing necklace or bracelet around the stem of a glass, securing it with glue on either end.

This cool effect does need some warning. The chemicals inside a glow stick are nasty (read more here) so be sure that the sticks you use are not leaking before placing them in a drink. The other point - and I would hope this would go without saying - is, please rinse the sticks before putting them in anyone's drinks... it's simple sanitation.

Creating Fog

Dry ice is an ideal way to add a foggy atmosphere to a party and is perfect for use on a drink table or display.

A classic way to incorporate dry ice is to use it under a punch bowl illuminated by black lights. There are also these great dry ice ideas from About.com Chemistry Guide, Anne Helmenstine. The foggy drink and punch bowl hands are two of my favorites. Though it may be a neat effect, not everyone (myself included) enjoys dry ice directly in their drink.

A unique dry ice idea comes from Nick Tether's La Dame Blasee cocktail. He uses dry ice as an aromatic back to the absinthe and vodka cocktail. A similar foggy cup could be used to compliment almost any cocktail.

THANKSGIVING

Thanksgiving is the holiday that sets off the wintertime holiday season, and the Christmas rush to get presents, food, and everything else people need to get through to January. For those throwing parties for friends and/or family, here are some themed cocktails sure to amuse your guests.

If Tom the Turkey doesn't bring Thanksgiving thoughts to mind, I don't know what does. Eith a bottle of Wild Turkey, these creations become possible.

Turkey Trot
2 cups Cranberry juice
2 cups 7-Up
1 cup Wild Turkey

Mix with a stirrer in a pitcher then pour over ice into glasses.

Turkeyball
1 oz Wild Turkey

3/4 oz Amaretto
1 splash Pineapple juice

Shake with ice and strain into a shot glass.

Almost as synonymous with the holiday is cranberry sauce with your turkey! So here are some Cranberry drinks. The Cordial will take prep time though - 6 weeks!

Cranberry Cordial
1/2 kg coarsely chopped Cranberries
3/4 L Sugar
1/2 L Light rum

Place the chopped cranberries in a 2 liter jar that has a tight-fitting lid. Add the sugar and rum. Adjust the lid securely and place the jar in a cool, dark place. Invert the jar and shake it every day for six weeks. Strain the cordial into bottles and seal with corks.

Crantini

1 1/2 oz Vodka
1/2 oz Triple sec
1/2 oz Vermouth
4 oz Cranberry juice
Ice cubes
Cranberries (optional)

Add all the ingredients in a martini shaker with ice. Then shake, pour into martini glass and add a few cranberries to complete the drink.(Soak the cranberries in vodka first)

Even in mid-September, pumpkins are being used as decorations. Pumpkin pie is a favorite Thanksgiving dessert, and these won't leave you disappointed.

Pumpkin Eater
1 1/2 oz Light rum

1 oz Orange Curacao
1/2 oz Triple sec
1 oz Orange juice
1/2 oz Cream

Add ice and ingredients into blender and blend well. Serve in a house glass and garnish with a orange wedge and cherry.

Pumpkin Pie
2 parts Kahlua
1 part Bailey's Irish cream
1 part Goldschlager
Cinnamon

After adding the Goldschlager, set on fire. Sprinkle cinnamon on the flame to "cook" and for dramatic effect. Blow out and serve.

And for the general Thanksgiving drinks, try the following.

Thanksgiving Cocktail
1 1/2 oz Wild Turkey
1/2 oz Applejack
1 tsp Rose's sweetened lime juice
4 oz Cranberry juice

Fill glass one-half full of ice, add ingredients and stir. Garnish with a lime wedge, if desired

NEW YEAR'S EVE

Orange-Cherry Champagne Cocktails

In China, citrus is given at the New Year as a sign of prosperity. In a champagne cocktail, sweet-tart oranges balance the flavors of the alcohol and other fruit.

Ingredients:
3 seedless oranges, halved and juiced
Peel of 1/2 orange, cut into 8 thin strips, for garnish
1/2 cup(s) red cherries, pitted
1/2 cup(s) sweet vermouth (such as Carpano Antica)
1/4 cup(s) blended Scotch (such as Famous Grouse)
1 bottle(s) champagne or other dry sparkling wine (such as Domaine Saint Vincent Brut), chilled

Directions
1.Transfer orange juice to a blender. Add cherries and blend until fruit is pureed. Strain juice into a pitcher. Stir in vermouth and Scotch.
2.Divide cocktail mixture among 8 glasses and top off each with about 1/3 cup champagne. Garnish with orange peels.

4rth of JULY
Patriotic Drink

Here's the trick to pouring a refreshing red, white, and blue summer drink

With a steady hand and some colorful drinks, you can create a tasty, multilayered concoction. The secret is in selecting liquids with varying amounts of sugar, since those that contain more (such as soda) are denser than those with less (such as diet drinks). And that makes it possible to actually stack one on top of another (for a little while, anyway -- then they'll start to blend). Here's how to serve up a thirst quencher with two, three, or even more layers. Our recipe is for a red, white, and blue version for your Fourth of July celebrations. See how your favorite beverages literally stack up!

What you'll need
Ice cubes
Cranberry juice
Wild Berry flavor Gatorade Fierce
Diet 7-Up

How to make it
1
Fill a clear glass with ice cubes. Pour the drink with the most sugar (check the nutrition label) into the glass. For our red, white, and blue recipe, start with the cranberry juice.

2
Very slowly add a beverage that contains less sugar -- in this case, Wild Berry flavor Gatorade Fierce. Be careful to pour it onto an ice cube -- not directly into the other drink -- to keep them from mixing.

3
Use the same technique to add a layer of Diet 7-Up.

Red, White and Blueberry Smoothie

This drink is the perfect treat for a Fourth of July breakfast or brunch. The layered red, white, and blue effect will get everyone in the holiday spirit.

This drink is the perfect treat for a Fourth of July breakfast or brunch. The layered red, white, and blue effect will get everyone in the holiday spirit.

What you'll need
1/2 cup vanilla flavored yogurt, plus more for garnish
2 cups fresh or frozen strawberries
1 cup milk or water
1 large banana, cut up
2 tablespoons sugar
1/2 cup blueberries, for garnish

Pour mixture into Popsicle molds and freeze for a delicious frozen treat.

Serves four

How to make it
Place yogurt, strawberries, milk, banana and sugar into a blender. Blend until smooth. Pour into tall glasses and top each drink with 1 teaspoon of yogurt and garnish with blueberries.

A
Abbey
1 ½ oz. gin
¾ oz orange juice
Dash of orange bitters

Shake well with ice. Strain into a cocktail glass with ice and garnish with a cherry.

Acapulco
1 ¾ oz. rum
¼ oz. Triple Sec
½ oz. lime juice
1 egg white
½ teaspoon superfine sugar
Mint leaves

Combine ingredients and shake well with ice. Strain into a cocktail or old-fashioned glass over ice. Partially tear the mint leaves and drop them into the drink.

A Hole in One
What makes a man a man? Why, his love of sport, of course. Order A Hole in One and you'll be oozing with the manly athleticism that sets you apart from the rest of the bar crowd.

Ingredients:
1 1/2 oz Johnnie Walker Red Label

1 tbsp honey
3 oz unsweetened tea
1 lemon wedge

How to prepare it: Add the Johnnie Walker Red Label, honey and unsweetened tea in a glass; stir it and serve over ice. Garnish the drink with a lemon wedge.

Akalei Fiasco
2 oz Rum
 2 1/2 oz Apple Juice
2 1/2 oz Orange Juice
1 oz Strawberry Daiquiri Mix
 Best served in a Cocktail Glass.

Add ingredients in any order to a cocktail glass packed with ice. Swivel and enjoy.

Alabama Slammer
1 oz Southern Comfort
1 oz Sloe Gin
Orange Juice to taste

Alice in Wonderland
•1 part Amaretto
•1 part Grand Marnier
•1 part Southern Comfort

Instructions
 Use an old fashioned glass, and add one part Amaretto, one part Grand Marnier, one part Southern Comfort

Amaretto Wine Spritzer
2 oz Amaretto
 1/2 Wine
1/2 soda

ice

Instructions
rocks Add 2 oz flavor mix or Schnapps for a Cherry, Peach, Blackberry, Raspberry, Strawberry, or Wildberry Amaretto Wine Spritzer

Apple Martini

A somewhat sour yet elegant drink which I consumed while on an extended stay in New York, you're sure to ask for a second!

1 part of absolut Vodka
1 part of DeKuper Sour apple Pucker Schnapps
1 part of apple juice

Pour all of the ingredients into a shaker, shake well and then strain into a martini glass.

Artic Red

4 cl finlandia cranberry vodka
4 tsp sugar
6 pieces lime peel
10 cl soda water
1 lime slice

First smash the limes and sugar to bottom of glass. Then add vodka and soda. Mix the drink with a spoon. Add ice cubes and lemon.

Attitude Adjustment

Ingredients
1/4 oz Vodka
1/4 oz Gin
1/4 oz Triple sec
1/4 oz Amaretto
1/4 oz Peach schnapps
1/4 oz Sour mix

1 splash Cranberry juice

Directions
Pour all ingredients into a mixing tin with ice, and strain into glass.

A Walk on the Moon
2 oz blackberry schnapps
1 oz vodka
3 oz cola
3 oz milk

Mix everything in a tall glass. Serve w/straw.

Aviation Cocktail
This classic cocktail was invented sometime around Prohibition, back when flying was a rare and wild thing.

Serves: 1
Ice
2 ounces gin
2 teaspoons maraschino liqueur
¾ ounce lemon juice
Add to favorites

1.Chill a martini glass in the freezer. Add ice to a cocktail shaker. Pour in the gin, maraschino liqueur and lemon juice. Shake and strain into chilled glass.

AWOL
1/2 oz amaretto almond liqueur
1 oz Scotch whisky
1/2 oz Orange Curacao liqueur
3/4 oz lime juice

Preparation Instructions:

Shake and strain into an old-fashioned glass filled with broken ice. Serve with a wedge of orange on the rim.

B
Back Seater
Scale ingredients to servings

1/2 oz brandy
1/2 oz apple brandy
1/2 oz triple sec
1 tsp lemon juice

Shake ingredients in a cocktail shaker with ice. Strain into a cocktail glass.

Backseat Boogie
3/4 oz vodka
3/4 oz gin
 fill with 1/2 ginger ale
 fill with 1/2 cranberry juice
 ice cubes

Pour Gin and Vodka over ice, followed by the cranberry juice and then the ginger ale.

Serve in: Highball Glass

- *Backseat Boogie #2 recipe*

1 oz Absolut® vodka
1 oz gin
1 part ginger ale
1 part Ocean Spray® cranberry juice

Pour vodka and gin over ice in a collins glass. Fill with equal parts of ginger ale and cranberry juice. Garnish with fruit, and serve.

Serve in: Collins Glass

Baha Fog
1 can Beer
6 oz Tequila
1/4 cup Lime

Baha Fog Mixing Directions
 Open a corona and fill it to the top with tequila. Squeeze a 1/4 lime on top. Chug immediately.

Balrog
Ingredients for a "Balrog"
•Vodka
•Tequila
•Sambuca

Quantities for one drink:
•1 Part/s Vodka
•1 Part/s Tequila
•1 Part/s Sambuca

Blending Instructions:
•Pour equal measures of each ingredient into 'one' shot glass, Drink, enjoy

Serving Glass: Shot Glass

Black Bitch (shot)
¾ oz Black Sambuca
¾ oz Bailey's irish cream
½ oz barcardi 151 proof rum

Layer Bailey's irish cream over Black Sambuca. Top with barcardi 151 rum.

Black cat
- 1.5 oz Old Forester Bourbon
- 1 oz Ginger ale
- 2 oz Cola
- Squeeze of lime
- Garnish with crushed lime wedge

1. In a highball glass, add first three ingredients
2. Squeeze lime wedge into glass and garnish with crushed lime wedge
3. Serve

BLACKHAWK
Ingredients:
- 1/2 oz. blackberry brandy
- 1/2 oz. lime juice
- 1 1/2 oz. vodka
- Lime slice

Mixing instructions:
Mix all ingredients, except lime slice, with cracked ice in a shaker or blender. Strain into a chilled cocktail glass and garnish with lime slice.

Black Russian
Scale ingredients to servings

3/4 oz coffee liqueur
1 1/2 oz vodka

Pour ingredients over ice cubes in an old-fashioned glass and serve.

B 52

Coffee and Irish cream liqueurs are a delicious combination and the addition of an orange liqueur gives this popular shot a slight fruity taste. The B-52 is also a great shot to practice your layering skills with. This also makes a great, thick sipping cocktail when the ingredients are increased, keeping the same ratio, shaken and served in a chilled cocktail glass.

Ingredients:
•1/2 oz coffee liqueur
•1/2 oz Irish cream liqueur
•1/2 oz orange liqueur (Grand Marnier)

1.Pour the coffee liqueur into a shot glass.
2.Float the Irish cream liqueur on top.
3.Float the Grand Marnier on top of the second layer.

Bloody Mary (New Version)

4 cups tomato juice (preferably Campbell's)
1 cup dill pickle juice
1/4 cup fresh lemon juice
1 tablespoon prepared horseradish
2 teaspoons Worcestershire sauce
2 teaspoons curry powder
1 teaspoon Sriracha
1 teaspoon kosher salt
1/2 teaspoon celery seeds
1/4 teaspoon black pepper
2 cups vodka
8 celery stalks
8 lemon wedges

Combine 4 cups tomato juice (preferably Campbell's), 1 cup dill pickle juice, 1/4 cup fresh lemon juice, 1 tablespoon prepared horseradish, 2 teaspoons Worcestershire sauce, 2 teaspoons curry powder, 1 teaspoon Sriracha, 1 teaspoon kosher salt, 1/2 teaspoon celery seeds, and 1/4 teaspoon black pepper in a large pitcher. Chill overnight. Add 2 cups vodka to pitcher; stir well. Fill tall glasses with ice. Divide Bloody Mary cocktail among glasses. Garnish each with a celery stalk and a lemon wedge.

Blow Job Shot

There are almost as many variations to this bachelorette party shot requirement as there are ways to blush while trying to order it at the bar.   You know how it goes...the most timid member of the group has to order the shot and the bartender 'pretends' not to hear the order four or five times until the poor girl is practically screaming for a Blow Job Shot above the rest of the crowd. The frivolity just doesn't stop since this shot requires the bride-to-be to find some tall, dark, handsome stranger to sit perfectly still while she places the Blow Job Shot between his knees and she takes the shot while on her knees without the use of her hands. The party just never stops... until that is the bride-to-be decides she wants a Screaming Orgasm, but that's really just another shot.

Blow Job Shot 1
1/4 part Coffee Liqueur
1/2 part Irish Cream
Whipped Cream Topper

Blow Job Shot 2
1/4 part Amaretto
1/2 part Coffee Liqueur
Whipped Cream Topper

Blow Job Shot 3
1 part Banana Liqueur

1 part Premium Orange Liqueur
1 part Coffee Liqueur
Whipped Cream Topper

Each recipe combines the same: Build in a shot glass in the order given. Top with a pile of whipped topping.

Blue Melon Balls (Shot)
1 part Hiram Walker Melon Liqueur
1 part Stoli Blueberi Vodka
Splash of lime juice

Shake with ice and serve in a shot glass.

Blue Moon Martini
1 1/2 oz Bombay Sapphire® gin
3/4 oz Blue Curacao liqueur

Shake with ice and strain into a cocktail glass. Garnish with a twist of lemon

BLUE SHARK
Ingredients:
•Several dashes blue curaçao
•3/4 oz. tequila
•3/4 oz. vodka

Mixing instructions:
Mix all ingredients with cracked ice in a blender or shaker and pour into a chilled Old Fashioned glass.

Boilermaker
2 oz whiskey
10 oz beer

Fill shot glass with whiskey. Drop full shot glass into mug o' beer. Drink immediately, enjoy.

Bourbon Slush

Ingredients
1 (6 ounce) can frozen orange juice concentrate
1 (12 ounce) can frozen lemonade concentrate
1 (46 fluid ounce) can pineapple juice
1 1/2 cups white sugar
2 cups strong brewed black tea
2 cups bourbon whiskey
1 (2 liter) bottle lemon-lime flavored carbonated beverage

Directions
1. In a large bowl or container, mix together the orange juice concentrate, lemonade concentrate, pineapple juice, sugar, tea, and whiskey. Transfer to shallow bowls or dishes, and freeze overnight.
2. Remove the frozen mixture from the freezer and let stand for about 10 minutes. Chop with a wire whisk or potato masher to make a slushy consistency. Place scoops of the frozen slush into glasses, and top off with the lemon-lime flavored soda.

Brass Monkey

1/2 oz rum
1/2 oz vodka
4 oz orange juice

Toss the rum and vodka together and stir gently. Pour in the orange juice, and shake well. Pour over ice in a highball or tall glass.

Buca Bord

½ oz. Sambvuca
½ oz. Chambord

Blend or stir and serve in a shot glass.

Burning Sun
Ingredients:
1 1/2 oz Strawberry schnapps
4 oz Pineapple juice
Mixing instructions:

Pour over ice in highball glass, stir. Garnish with a fresh strawberry

C
C & M
Scale ingredients to servings

2 oz Malibu® coconut rum
2 oz Stolichnaya® vanilla vodka
4 - 5 oz Coca-Cola®

Pour 2 oz. of malibu rum into a glass filled half way with ice

Proceed to pour in 2 oz. of Stoli Vanilla into the glass.

Fill the remainder of the glass with Coca Cola to the brim and enjoy

Cactus Cooler
3/4 oz triple sec
3/4 oz Absolut Mandrin vodka
8 oz Rockstar energy drink

Preparation Instructions:
 Fill a shot glass half with triple sec, half mandarin vodka; then drop into a pint glass half-filled with Rockstar energy drink, and serve.

Serve In:
beer mug

California Lemonaide

½ oz. gin
½ oz. vodka
½ oz. rum
½ oz. tequila
½ oz. triple sec
1 ½ oz sweetened lemon juice
7 Up

Fill a large tumbler with ice. Add all the ingredients except the 7 Up. STIR all together. Now add the 7 Up. Garnish with a wedge of lemon.

Captain Steamy

4 oz Apple cider
1/2 oz Captain Morgan's Spiced rum
1/2 oz Coconut rum (Parrot Bay)
1/2 oz Sour Apple Pucker

Directions:
Start with hot or steamed apple cider. Add equal parts apple schnapps, spiced rum and coconut rum. Stir. This very tasty, and warms-you-from-the-inside-out adult beverage started with a request for Spiced Apple Rum at a holiday party. The bartender's interpretation of Captain Morgan's was Captain Morgan's 'Parrot Bay' vs. the spiced rum our favorite pirate is known for. We added the remaining ingredients anyway, and voila--a star is born.

Cherry Bomb

Ingredients:
1 oz Vodka
1 1/2 oz Creme de Cacao
3/4 oz Grenadine
Mixing instructions:
Serve as a shot or on the rocks

Cherry Drop (Shot)

Cherry Drop Ingredients
◦1/2 oz Aftershock Hot & Cool cinnamon schnapps
◦1/2 oz Kahlua coffee liqueur

Cherry Drop Mixing Directions
Shake ingredients in a cocktail shaker with ice. Strain into a large shot glass. Add a maraschino cherry without a stem to the middle of the shot.

Serve In: Shot Glass

Cherry Popper

1/2 Banana
Crushed Ice
1/2 Orange Slice
4 Vodka
4 Water

Preparation Instructions:
Cut the banana and orange into halves then put them in the blender with approx. 10 cubes of ice and 4 oz of water. Put the lid on the blender, after that add the 4 oz of vodka, blend slowly until well blended and serve in a highball glass. Garnish with a cherry.

Serve In:
highball glass

City Slicker

2 oz brandy
1/2 oz triple sec
1 tbsp lemon juice

Preparation Instructions:
In a shaker half-filled with ice cubes, combine all of the ingredients. Shake well. Strain into a cocktail glass.

Serve In:
cocktail glass

Cock 'n Balls

1 oz Smirnoff Watermelon Twist
1 oz Smirnoff Green Apple Twist
5 oz Raspberry Lemonade

Pour the raspberry lemonade into a highball glass with several ice cubes. Add the vodka's by stirring in as you pour, and serve.

Serve Cock 'n Balls in a Highball Glass

Colorado Rattlesnake

1 1/2 oz chilled Tequila
1 1/2 oz Tomato juice
1-4 dash Tabasco sauce
1-4 dash Black pepper

Directions
Pour chilled Tequila in shoot glass and put to the side. Pour Tomato Juice in a second shot glass and dash pepper and Tabasco in the Tomato Juice. Shoot Tequila and chase with tomato juice shot.

Commando Cocktail

1 1/2 oz bourbon whiskey
3/4 oz triple sec
2 dashes Pernod licorice liqueur
3/4 oz lime juice

Preparation Instructions:

Pour the bourbon whiskey, triple sec, pernod and lime juice into a cocktail shaker half-filled with ice cubes. Shake well, strain into a cocktail glass, and serve.
Serve In:
collins glass

Cosmopolitan

1 oz vodka
1/2 oz triple sec
1/2 oz Rose's® lime juice
1/2 oz cranberry juice

Shake vodka, triple sec, lime and cranberry juice vigorously in a shaker with ice. Strain into a martini glass, garnish with a lime wedge on the rim, and serve.

Cosmopolitan Slushy

10 ounce (1 1/4 cups) citrus-flavored vodka
1/2 cup Rose's lime juice
2 cups cranberry juice
4 ice cube trays

Directions
1.Combine vodka, lime juice, and cranberry juice in a pitcher with 2 cups water and stir to blend. Divide between ice cube trays and freeze at least 4 hours or overnight (the drink cubes will freeze only partially).
2.Just before serving, empty trays into a large bowl and using a fork, break up cubes to loosen ice crystals (the ice will be slushlike). Spoon slush into tall stemmed glasses and serve immediately.

COYOTE

Ingredients:
- 1.5 oz Tequila
- 1.5 oz. Goldschlager
- 4.5 oz Club Soda
- 5-7 drops Hot Sauce

Directions:
Pour all ingredients into a glass with ice, stir and serve.

Crack Pipe

1 oz Bacardi 151 rum
1 oz Rumple Minze peppermint liqueur
1 oz Wild Turkey bourbon whiskey

Preparation Instructions: Shake with ice, strain into glass.

Crazy Dave

1/2 oz Skyy vodka
1/4 oz Bacardi gold rum
1/4 oz sweet and sour mix
1/4 oz Bacardi 151 rum
1/2 oz cosmopolitan mix

Preparation Instructions:

Pour all ingredients into a cocktail shaker half-filled with ice cubes. Shake well, strain into a double-shot glass, and serve.

Cuba Libre

Serves: 1
1 lime, juiced
Ice
2 ounces white rum
Coca-Cola

1.Add lime juice and ice to a cocktail glass. Pour in rum and cola. Stir and garnish with a slice of lime.

Cucumber Saketini

Ingredients
3 ounces gin
1/2 ounce sake
5 thin slices of cucumber

Directions
1.In a shaker with ice, mix together the gin and sake. Strain into a martini glass and garnish with the cucumber.

D
Daffy Duck

Daffy Duck Ingredients
∘1 oz Vodka
∘3 oz White Wine

Daffy Duck Mixing Directions
 Combine ingredients in a wine glass, and serve.

Serve In:
White Wine Glass

Dancing Bones

1 1/2 oz dry vermouth
2 tsp gin
2 tsp cherry brandy

Preparation Instructions:
 Pour vermouth, gin and cherry brandy into a mixing glass half-filled with ice cubes, and stir. Strain into a cocktail glass, and serve.

Dancing Dutchman

25 tsp vodka
5 cups ice cubes
5 cups strawberry juice
1 cup white wine
1 cup lime juice
3 cups peach juice
15 tsp Scotch whisky
 rum

Mix fruit juices together in one bowl, place in blender with ice cubes. When slushy mixture is complete, stir in alcohol and shake until completly mixed. Place mixture in punchbowl, and float cherries in the bowl if desired.

Dante's Inferno
1 1/2 oz Stoli® Strasberi vodka
3/4 oz Marie Brizard® watermelon liqueur
2 splashes 7-Up® soda
2 - 3 squirts chocolate syrup

Take a martini glass and rim with sugar. Then, draw a pentagram in the glass with the chocolate syrup. Combine the liquor and one splash of 7up over ice and shake. Pour carefully into the very center of the martini glass to not upset the syrup design. When finished, add another splash of 7up for effervescence. Garnish with a chocolate covered strawberry and serve.

Deep 7
1 1/2 oz amaretto almond liqueur
1 1/2 oz coconet rum
6 oz 7 up soda

Pour in amaretto and rum on the rocks then add 7 up. Stir and serve.

Dirty Dog
1 oz Hennessy Cognac
1 ½ oz vodka
5 oz orange juice
1 oz cranberry juice

Mix and serve over ice in an old fashioned glass

Double Jack   (Shot)

Double Jack Ingredients
 1/2 shot Bourbon
1/2 shot Yukon Jack

Double Jack Mixing Directions
 Combine the two jacks in glass.

Dreamcatcher

1 1/2 oz Absolut® vodka
1/2 oz Gordon's® gin
2 oz Bols® Blue Curacao liqueur
2 splashes Rose's® lime juice
2 splashes lime juice
1/2 oz Rose's® grenadine syrup
1 - 2 oz 7-Up® soda

Build over ice, pour the shot of vodka in first and then layer the shooter of blue curacao on top of that. Splash the gin over the curaco and add the lime cordial, after this fill the glass up with 7-up and squeeze some lime juice in there. Drop the grenadine in last, to keep it deep purple at the bottom just don't stir it, this makes for a stronger drink.

Drummer Shot (Shot)

1/2 oz Jagermeister herbal liqueur
1/2 oz Bacardi 151 rum

Mix ingredients in shot glass and prepare to be tough.

Dutch Coffee

Scale ingredients to servings

1 oz oude genever gin
5 ozhot black coffee
1 1/2 oz whipped cream
1 tsp sugar

Pour coffee and liquor into an irish coffee cup and sweeten to taste. Gently float the cream on top, and sprinkle with nutmeg.

E

Eastern Sour

°2 oz bourbon whiskey
°1 oz lime juice
°1 1/2 oz orange juice
°1/4 oz orgeat syrup
°1/4 oz sugar syrup

Eastern Sour Mixing Directions
Shake all ingredients with ice. Strain into an ice-filled old fashioned glass. Garnish with lime wedge.
Serve In:

Old-Fashioned Glass

Electric Lemonade

¾ oz curacao
¾ oz Rum
2 oz Sweet & Sour Mix
Splash Lemon Lime Soda

Pour all ingredients layer after layer in a Collins glass. Garnish with a lemon wedge. Serve with a straw.

El Nino

1 oz vodka
1 oz peach schnapps
1/2 oz Blue Curacao liqueur
2 oz pineapple juice
2 oz orange juice
1 splash soda water

Mix all ingredients in a shaker with ice and shake vigorously. Strain over ice in a hurricane glass, and garnish with a pineapple wedge and a cherry.

English Pirate

6 oz Bacardi® light rum
12 ozsweetened iced tea
6 ice cubes

In a large (20 oz or larger) mug or mason jar, pour in rum and fill to within 1 inch of top with sweetened iced tea. Add ice and enjoy. Lemon can be added to taste.

Exploding Cherry

Exploding Cherry Ingredients
 ○1/2 bottle Vodka
○5 slices Pineapple
○1/4 bottle Coconut Liqueur
○3 splashes Fruit Juice

Exploding Cherry Mixing Directions
 Pour it all into an ice-cream pail and add more vodka if you wish.

Serve In: Pitcher

Eyes Wide Shut
Scale ingredients to servings

1/2 oz Southern Comfort® peach liqueur
1/2 oz Crown Royal® Canadian whisky
1/2 oz amaretto almond liqueur
1/2 oz orange juice
1/2 oz pineapple juice
1/2 oz cranberry juice
1 splash grenadine syrup

Place ice in shaker and add all ingredients. Shake well and strain into cocktail glass filled with ice. Garnish with orange slice and cherry.

F

Fahrenheit 151 recipe

This cocktail was concieved by adding the idea of a classic rum and coke with the growing popularity of energy drinks/alcohol. The product was the Fahrenheit 151, whose title was derived from the famous novel, Fahrenheit 451. There really isn't a relation between the two, but the name is catchy. Enjoy!

Scale ingredients to servings
4 oz Bacardi® 151 rum
4 oz Red Bull® energy drink
8 oz Coca-Cola®

First, add the Bacardi 151 into the Collins glass. Then, pour the half can of Red Bull, and proceed to add about 4 or 5 pieces of ice. Fill the rest of the glass with Coca-Cola and serve.

Fat Box (Shot)
1/4 oz creme de bananes
1/4 oz Blue Curacao liqueur

1/4 oz Malibu coconut rum
1/2 oz pineapple juice

Preparation Instructions: Pour all ingredients into a ice filled shaker. Shake until chilled then strain into a shot glass.

Fat Cat
Scale ingredients to servings
1 oz Bailey's® Irish cream
1/2 oz amaretto almond liqueur
1/2 oz banana liqueur

Fill mixing cup 1/4 full with ice. Add all three ingredients. Shake and strain into a shot glass or serve on the rocks.

Fat Charley recipe
Scale ingredients to servings

1 oz Bacardi® white rum
1 oz Malibu® coconut rum
1 oz 99 Bananas® banana schnapps
5 oz orange juice
1 splash cranberry juice

Pour the Bacardi rum, Malibu rum and 99 Bananas into a collins glass filled with ice cubes. Fill with orange juice, adding a splash of cranberry juice to top. Stir and serve.

Fat Frog
The drink Fat Frog is a fruity combination of 3 of Europe's most popular selling 5% "alcopops" or malt-beverages. It's therefore most popular in Europe, namely Britain and British holiday destinations where the ingredients are more widely available.

1 bottle Smirnoff® Ice
1 bottle Bacardi Breezer® Orange
1 bottle WKD® Original Vodka Blue

Get 2 pint glasses, pour one half of Smirnoff Ice into one pint glass and the rest in the other glass, then do the same with the orange breezer, then followed by the Blue WKD. Mix, and the drink should turn green. Add ice as desired, and serve.

Fire and Ice
Fire and Ice Ingredients
○1/2 shot Rumple Minze
○1/2 shot Firewater

Fire and Ice Mixing Directions. Layer the rumple minze on top of the firewater. (as best as possible)

Serve In:

Highball Glass

Firecracker
•1 Schnapps
•1 Cherry Brandy
•Dash of Tabasco and Cinnamon
 Mix and Serve

Fire Shot recipe (Shot)
3/4 oz Chivas Regal® Scotch whisky
1 1/4 oz sambuca
1 drop grenadine syrup

Layer the ingredients in order of: Sambuca then scotch, then carefully place a drop of grenadine in the middle.

Flaming Blue Jesus

Ingredients
1 oz Bacardi 151 rum
1/2 oz peppermint schnapps
1/2 oz Southern Comfort peach liqueur
1/2 oz tequila

Directions
Layer with 151 proof rum on top. Light on fire - burn for 5 seconds - blow it out and drink.

Flaming Ho

Scale ingredients to servings

20 ml Midori® melon liqueur
10 ml tequila
 dried prune flakes
1/4 tspcrushed brown sugar

Take a shot glass and add the brown sugar and the flakes of dried prune. Fill the glass with 2/3 Midori melon liqueur and 1/3 tequila. Ignite it, let it burn for about 10 seconds and then blow out the flame. Bottoms up!

Flaming Russian (Shot)

Flaming Russian Ingredients
 ◦1/5 oz Vodka

Flaming Russian Mixing Directions
 Pour vodka in shot glass, carefully layer rum on top. Ignite rum and serve.

Flatliner

1 jigger sambuca
1 shot gold tequila
3 dashes Tabasco sauce

Directions
Layer the tequila over sambuca. Add tabasco sauce.

Freddy Kruger (Shot)

Ingredients for a "Freddy Kruger"
•Jägermeister
•Sambuca
•Vodka

Quantities for one drink:
•1/2 oz Jägermeister
•1/2 oz Sambuca
•1/2 oz Vodka

Blending Instructions:
•make it an ample size shot!!

Serving Glass: Shot Glass

French Kiss

1 oz vodka
1 oz raspberry liqueur
1/2 oz Grand Marnier orange liqueur
1 oz whipping cream

Directions
Shake and strain into a champagne flute. Garnish with a
speared cherry or raspberry, and serve.

Full Moon

Scale ingredients to servings

1 1/2 oz Orange Curacao liqueur
1 1/2 oz amaretto almond liqueur

Pour above ingredients into an ice-filled rocks glass, and serve.

Fuzzy Navel

1 1/2 oz. Peach Schnapps & Orange Juice
Mix and serve

G

G Bomb

1/2 shot Goldschlager cinnamon schnapps
1/2 shot Absolut vodka

Preparation Instructions:
Chill both ingredients by placing the bottles in the freezer for at least 1 hour. You should also chill the shot glasses you will be using the same way. Pour both ingredients into a chilled shot glass and enjoy.

Gibson

Simple and elegant, it's a gin martini where a cocktail onion replaces the olive.

Serves: 1

Ice
2 ounces gin
1/2 ounce dry vermouth
Cocktail onion for garnish
Add to favorites

1.Chill a martini glass in the freezer. Place ice in a cocktail pitcher or shaker. Pour gin and dry vermouth into the shaker or pitcher. Shake or stir to mix. Strain into a chilled martini glass. Garnish with a cocktail onion (or two).

Gingerbread Man
Scale ingredients to servings

1 part Kahlua® coffee liqueur
1 part Bailey's® Irish cream
1 part Goldschlager® cinnamon schnapps

Layer in sequence in a shot glass.

Ginger Shandies
During a stay in Texas, I had the chance to try this drink:
Ingredients:
3 bottle(s) (11.2-ounce) chilled Hoegaarden beer
1 bottle(s) (12-ounce) chilled ginger beer
1 thinly sliced lemon
Mint sprigs, for garnish

1.In a large pitcher, combine Hoegaarden with ginger beer. Stir in most lemon slices and mint sprigs. Fill 6 rocks glasses with ice. Add remaining lemon slices to glasses and pour in shandy. Garnish each drink with a mint sprig and serve

Gladiator

- 1/2 oz. Amaretto
- 1/2 oz. Southern Comfort
- Fill, 1/2 7-up
- Fill, 1/2 Orange Juice

Mixing Instructions:

In a shot glass, combine 1/2 oz. Amaretto and 1/2 oz. Southern Comfort. Place shot glass in a highball glass. Fill half-way to shot glass with 7-Up, fill to just below top of shot glass with Orange Juice. Shoot it.

Go-Go Girl

1 1/2 oz Bacardi® light rum
1 1/2 oz mango nectar
3 1/2 oz pineapple juice

Fill a highball glass with ice. Add rum and mango nectar. Top off glass with pineapple juice. Stir. Garnish with a slice of pineapple, and serve.

Gorilla Sweat Drink

2 oz Tequila
6 oz Water
1 tsp Butter
3 pieces Cloves
1 stick Cinnamon
1 pinch Salt (Optional

Directions
Mix all ingredients (except cinnamon stick) and heat gently until butter is melted. Garnish with cinnamon stick.

Grasshopper

3/4 oz green creme de menthe
3/4 oz white creme de cacao
3/4 oz light cream

Shake all ingredients with ice, strain into a cocktail glass, and serve.

Serve in: Cocktail Glass

Green Card (Shot)

Green Card Ingredients
 ∘3/4 oz Grey Goose vodka
 ∘3/4 oz Maker's Mark bourbon whiskey
 ∘1/4 oz Cointreau orange liqueur
 ∘1/4 oz Rose's blue raspberry mixer

Green Card Mixing Directions
 Pour the Grey Goose vodka into a double-shot glass. Add the Makers Mark bourbon whiskey, the Cointreau orange liqueur and Rose's infused blue raspberry mixer (the mixture should turn a dirty green); serve.

Serve In:

Shot Glass

Green Devil

Scale ingredients to servings

1 - 1/2 oz gin
1 oz green creme de menthe
1/2 oz lime juice

Shake all ingredients with ice and strain into an old-fashioned glass over a few ice cubes.

Green Fairy Blood

1 oz absinthe herbal liqueur
1 oz creme de menthe
1 oz Green Chartreuse
1 oz fresh water
1 tsp sugar

Directions :
Mix ingredients in above order over a sugar cube on an absinthe spoon, light the cube and when the flame dies immediately stir in the sugar until it dissolves; serve.

Green Vodka

 2 oz Vodka
4 oz 7-Up
6 oz Lemon-Lime Kool-Aid

Mix and drink.
Serve In:Collins Glass

Gypsy Cocktail

Scale ingredients to servings

1 1/2 oz sweet vermouth
1 1/2 oz gin
1 cherry

Stir gin and vermouth with ice and strain into a cocktail glass. Add the cherry on top and serve.

H

Hawaiian Sunset

Ingredients:
1 1/2 oz Vodka
2 1/2 oz Cranberry juice
2 1/2 oz Orange juice
1 1/2 oz Soda water
Mixing instructions:
Put ice cubes in the glass. Shake vodka, orange juice and cranberry juice in shaker. Poor into glass. Top off with soda water. Garnish with cherry and pinapple slice (optional).

Hairy Ass

2 oz Yukon Jack Canadian whisky
2 oz Crown Royal Canadian whisky
1 oz peach schnapps
3 oz Dr. Pepper soda

Directions
Pour the liquors into a blender with one cup of crushed ice. Blend well, and pour into a collins glass. Top with soda, and serve.

Happy Juice

Scale ingredients to servings

1 1/2 oz Malibu® coconut rum
1 1/2 oz peach schnapps
1/2 oz Ceres® guava juice
1/2 oz Looza mango nectar
1 oz pineapple juice
1 splash Ceres® passion-fruit juice

Combine the schnapps and Malibu rum in a highball glass; add in the pineapple juice. Add in the mango nectar and guava juice til the taste is suitable (may want to go light on the guava juice for its heavy distinctive taste) then top off with a splash of passion fruit juice, and serve.

Harvey Wall Banger
An old drink invented in 1952 that I consumed in the wilds of downtown Boston with two nameless chicks. But if you are in an old style mood, give it a try and make it a Harvey Wall Banger Night.

In a highball glass and garnished with orange slice and maraschino cherry:

4.5 cl (3 parts) vodka
1.5 (1 part) Galiano
9 cl (6 parts) fresh orange juice

stir vodka and orange juice with ice in glass then float the galliano on top, garnish and serve.

Hemingway Special
2 oz white rum
1/4 oz maraschino liqueur
 juice of 1/2 limes
1 oz grapefruit juice

Squeeze lime juice into a shaker, add remaining ingredients and shake briefly with a glassful of crushed ice. Serve in a frosted cocktail glass.

High Ball
Whiskey 1 ½ oz
Ginger ale to top
Lemon peel garnish

Preparation:
Fill a highball glass with ice. Add the Whiskey and top with the ginger ale. Gently stir and garnish.

Holy Water
Scale ingredients to servings

2 oz vodka
1 oz triple sec
1 oz light rum
 fill with tonic water
1 dash grenadine syrup

Combine alcohol in a rocks glass over ice. Fill with tonic water, then add one dash of grenadine. Be sure the drink is served with the tonic still bubbling.

HOT BULL (Shot)
Ingredients:
•Several dashes TABASCO® Brand Pepper Sauce
•Several dashes Worcestershire sauce
•3 oz. beef consommé
 or bouillon •3 oz. Tomato juice
 or V-8 juice •1 1/2 oz. vodka
 or tequila •Pinch celery seed
 or celery salt •Dash lemon juice
•Dash white pepper

Mixing instructions:
Heat all ingredients in a saucepan until steaming, but do not boil. Serve in a warmed, heat- proof mug.

Hot Frenchman
4 oz red wine
3/4 oz Grand Marnier orange liqueur
1/2 tsp sugar
1/4 oz orange juice
1/4 oz lemon juice
1 twist orange peel
1 twist lemon peel

Preparation Instructions:
Heat well in a heat-resistant glass or cup. Stir, add twists of lemon and orange peel, and serve in a cup.

Hunch Punch
1 gal Fruit Punch
1 bottle Everclear
1 jigger Fruit

Put them all together and mix it with a lot of ice. For big parties use more of each and mix in a garbage can.

Hulk (The)
1/3 cup abolut
1/3 cup cherry vodka
1 pack of grape kool-aid mix
1/2 cup of n.o. explode

mix all

Hummingbird

An alcoholic drink served in Jamaica. Contains rum cream liqueur, coffee liqueur, strawberry syrup, banana, and milk and ends up having a smoothie consistency

Ingredients

1 fluid ounce rum cream liqueur
1 fluid ounce coffee flavored liqueur
1 fluid ounce milk
1/2 fluid ounce strawberry flavored syrup
1/2 banana
1 cup crushed ice

Directions

1. In a blender, combine rum cream liqueur, coffee liqueur, milk and strawberry syrup. Add the banana and crushed ice. Blend until smooth. Pour into glasses and serve.

Hurricane

1 oz vodka
1/4 oz grenadine syrup
1 oz gin
1 oz light rum
1/2 oz Bacardi® 151 rum
1 oz amaretto almond liqueur
1 oz triple sec
 grapefruit juice
 pineapple juice

Pour all but the juices, in order listed, into a hurricane glass three-quarters filled with ice. Fill with equal parts of grapefruit and pineapple juice, and serve.

Serve in: Hurricane Glass

Hurricane, New Orleans Style

1 oz white rum
1 oz Jamaican dark rum

1 oz Bacardi® 151 rum
3 oz orange juice
3 oz unsweetened pineapple juice
1/2 oz grenadine syrup
 crushed ice

Combine all ingredients, mix well (shake or stir). Pour over crushed ice in hurricane glass. Best enjoyed through a small straw. Garnish with fruit wedge if desired.

Serve in: Hurricane Glass

I

I.B.U. recipe
Scale ingredients to servings

3/4 oz cognac
3/4 oz orange juice
1/4 oz apricot brandy
4 oz Champagne

Shake all ingredients (except champagne) over ice cubes in a shaker, and strain into a champagne flute. Fill with champagne, and serve.

Iceball
1 1/2 oz gin
3/4 oz sambuca
3/4 oz white creme de cacao
2 - 3 tsp cream

Add ingredients and 3 oz. crushed ice to blender. Blend on medium speed for about 15 seconds, until smooth. Pour into glass.

Iceberg

1/2 oz Peppermint Schnapps
1 oz Creme de Menthe
1/2 oz Goldschlager
(Fill to Top) Milk

Best served in a Highball Glass.

Pour ingredients over ice in a blender, blend, and pour into a frozen highball glass. Garnish with a cinnamon stick or chocolate shavings. More info on how to make a Iceberg

Iguana

Scale ingredients to servings

1/2 oz vodka
1/2 oz tequila
1/4 oz coffee liqueur
1 1/2 oz sweet and sour mix
1/2 slice lime

Shake all ingredients (except lime slice) with ice and strain into a chilled cocktail glass. Add the lime slice and serve.

Ink Drop (Shot)

Ink Drop Ingredients
 ○1/2 oz Captain Morgan Tattoo orange rum
 ○1 oz Red Bull energy drink

Ink Drop Mixing Directions
 Mix chilled Captain Morgan Tattoo rum with your favorite energy drink in a shot glass.

Irish's Cream Liqueur

2 Eggs
1 1/3 cups Evaporated milk
1/2 teaspoon Chocolate syrup
1 teaspoon Vanilla
1/3 teaspoon Lemon ext
1/4 teaspoon Instant coffee
1 3/4 cups Irish whiskey

Instructions
Place all ingredients in a blender; blend well. Bottle and let mellow in frig at least one week before serving. We found this best after 1 to 2 weeks. Store in frig. liqueur may be served at room temp by removing from frig an hour or two before serving

J

Jack Hammer
Scale ingredients to servings
1 oz vodka
1 oz Irish cream
1 oz peppermint schnapps
 top with milk

Pour the vodka, irish cream and peppermint schnapps into a collins glass filled with ice cubes. Top with milk, to taste, and serve.

Jack Hammer (Shot)
Scale ingredients to servings
1 oz Jack Daniel's® Tennessee whiskey
1 oz Jose Cuervo® Especial gold tequila

Pour both shots into one shot glass, straight up.

Jack the Ripper

Scale ingredients to servings

2 1/2 oz Crown Royal® Canadian whisky
3/4 oz butterscotch schnapps

Level ice to the top in a shaker, add crown royal and buttershots, then shake. Strain into a brandy snifter.

Jack Sauce (Shot)

Jack Sauce Ingredients
 ◦1/2 oz Jack Daniel's Tennessee whiskey
◦1/2 oz Bailey's Irish cream
◦1/2 oz amaretto almond liqueur
◦1 oz whipped cream

Jack Sauce Mixing Directions
 Pour into a shot glass in order. Top with whipped cream and serve!

Jack Sour

Scale ingredients to servings

2 oz Jack Daniel's® Tennessee whiskey
1 dash cherry juice
3 oz sweet and sour mix

Stir ingredients together in a cocktail glass, garnish with a cherry and an orange slice.

Jamaica Fever

3/4 oz brandy
1 1/2 oz dark rum
1 1/2 oz pineapple juice
3/4 oz mango syrup
3/4 oz lemon juice

Directions
Shake well over crushed ice in a shaker, and pour into a large highball glass over crushed ice. Add a pineapple chunk and a stemmed cherry, and serve.

Jamaican Mudslide

Serves: 4
16 ounces Dr Pepper(R)
1 cup crushed ice
1/2 cup pina colada mix
4 ounces rum (optional)
Add to favorites

1.Pour ice, pina colada mix, and rum into a blender and mix it for 10 minutes, alternating between ice crush, frappe, and mix, or until smooth, with no icy chunks. pour even amounts into 4 glasses. Pour 4 ounces of Dr Pepper into each of the four glasses.

Japanese Slipper

1 part Midori® melon liqueur
1 part Cointreau® orange liqueur
1 part lime juice

Combine equal parts of each ingredient in a cocktail glass. Stir, and serve.

Serve in: Cocktail Glass

Jello Shots (Shot)

2 packages Gelatin (flavor of choice)

1 cup Vodka

Mix gelatin according to package instructions, except substitute vodka for the cold water in process. Use small plastic cups for forming gelatin into shots. Place in refrigerator or freezer. Whipped topping optional garnish for fun just before serving.

Jello shots are a party favorite especially around St. Patrick's Day. Lime becomes the flavor of the day with the green theme. Other Jello Shot favorite gelatin flavors from Twitter and Facebook Q&A: Black Cherry, Blue Mixed Berry, Pineapple, Red and Orange.

John Collins Cocktail

You may know John's cousin, Tom. This one uses whiskey instead of gin.

Serves: 1
Ice
2 ounces bourbon or rye whiskey
½ ounce fresh lemon juice
1 teaspoon sugar
Club soda
Slice of lemon for garnish

1.Fill a tall cocktail glass with ice. Pour in whiskey and lemon juice. Stir in sugar to dissolve. Top with club soda and garnish with a slice of lemon

Jock Strap
Scale ingredients to servings

3 oz vodka
13 oz Gatorade® orange soda

Combine ingredients in a collins glass.

Jonesey
Scale ingredients to servings

2 oz dark rum
1/2 oz dark creme de cacao

In a mixing glass half-filled with ice cubes, combine the rum and creme de cacao. Stir well. Strain into a cocktail glass.

Johnny Cat
1 oz gin
1 oz dry vermouth
1/2 oz triple sec
1 swirl grenadine syrup
 fill with club soda
4 ice cubes

Preparation Instructions:
 Place gin or vodka, triple sec, vermouth, grenadine and ice into a shaker. Shake well and pour into a red wine glass. Fill with tonic water or club soda.

Serve In:
red wine glass

Joy Ride

1 1/4 oz Absolut Citron vodka
3/4 oz Campari bitters
3 oz sweet and sour mix
2 lemons wedges
1 tbsp sugar
soda water

Directions
Muddle lemon and sugar in a mixing glass. Add ice, absolut citron, campari and sweet and sour. Shake well and dump into a hurricane glass. Spritz with soda.

K

Kamaikaze

No party would be complete without this stiff drink to zip through the night with friends.

1) 1.25 oz Vodka
2) .25 oz triple sec
3) .25oz lime juice

add lime juice, triple sec and vodka. Shake and strain into a shot glass

King Kong recipe

Scale ingredients to servings

2 oz light rum
1 maraschino cherry
1/2 banana
1 tsp nutmeg
1 oz banana liqueur
8 oz ice
1 oz Malibu® coconut rum
1 splash orange juice
3 oz pineapple juice
2 tbsp 151 proof rum
1/2 can cream of coconut

Add all ingredients to a blender, and combine on medium power for 45 seconds. Serve in a pitcher with a cute umbrella and a straw.

Kiss Goodnight (A)

1 1/2 oz DeKuyper® Raspberry Pucker schnapps
1 1/2 oz strawberry vodka
3 - 4 oz 7-Up® soda
3 - 4 oz cranberry juice

Add strawberry vodka and raspberry pucker, then fill half way with cranberry juice. Fill the rest with 7-up and float a splash of dark rum on top

Knock-Out
Scale ingredients to servings

200 ml beer
30 ml white rum
30 ml dark rum
200 ml apple juice

Fill a 475ml glass with ice - about 1/4 of the way. Pour beer into glass. Pour white rum & dark rum into glass. Top-up with apple juice, and serve.

K.T.C.G. Special
1 shot vodka
1 shot hennessy
1 shot patron
1 shot crown royal
1 shot blue hawiian pucker
1 shot yeager
1 part cranapple juice
1 part sprite

Directions
Mix as directed and serve on the rock's

L

La Bomba
1 1/4 oz gold tequila
3/4 oz Cointreau® orange liqueur
1 1/2 oz pineapple juice
1 1/2 oz orange juice
2 dashes grenadine syrup

Shake all ingredients (except grenadine) with ice 3 times. Pour into sugar rimmed cocktail glass. Add grenadine and garnish with a lime wheel.

Lady Killer

Scale ingredients to servings
1 oz gin
1/2 oz Cointreau® orange liqueur
1/2 oz apricot brandy
2 oz passion-fruit juice
2 oz pineapple juice

Shake all ingredients with ice in shaker, strain into a champagne flute or longdrink glass over some ice cubes. Decorate with mint and a cherry.

Lava Flow

1 oz Light rum 1 oz Malibu rum 2 oz Strawberries 1 Banana 2 oz Pineapple juice 2 oz Coconut cream

Blend banana, coconut cream, and pineapple juice in blender and set aside. In bottom of hurricane glass, stir together both rums and strawberries. Pour banana/coconut/pineapple mix into glass slowly. The strawberry/rum mix should creep up the sides of the glass to make a wonderful looking (and tasting) summertime cocktail!

Lewd Lewinsky (Shot)

Lewd Lewinsky Ingredients
∘1/2 oz Jagermeister
∘1/2 oz Cream

Lewd Lewinsky Mixing Directions
 Layer in order.

Serve In: Shot Glass

Lime Avenger

2 oz lime vodka
6 oz Mountain Dew® citrus soda

Pour the lime vodka into a highball glass half-filled with ice cubes. Add the Mountain Dew, and serve.

Liquid Viagra

1 shot Jagermeister herbal liquor.
1/3 can Red Bull energy drink.
Pour Red Bull into a shot glass.
Add a shot of Jagermeister, including the shot glass into the Red Bull.
Shoot it down.

Long Island Taxi

A popular cocktail at the Lakewood Lounge, Kansas City, Mo, where Long Island Taxi originated via a guy named Matt.

Scale ingredients to servings

2 oz vodka
1 oz gin
1 oz tequila
1 oz rum
 orange juice

Pour all liquors into a cocktail shaker filled with ice. Add orange juice to taste, and shake. Strain into shot glasses or a single highball glass, and serve.

M

M&M (Shot)
1/2 oz Frangelico® hazelnut liqueur
1/2 oz creme de cacao

Serve straight up in a shot glass.

Mad Russian
◦1 oz vodka
◦1 oz Kahlua coffee liqueur
◦1/2 oz Bailey's Irish cream
◦1/2 oz butterscotch schnapps
◦5 - 6 oz milk

Mad Russian Mixing Directions
 Fill glass with ice, add 1 shot each of vodka and Kahlua and 1/2 shot each of Baileys and butterscotch and fill with milk. Shake or stir.

Serve in Hurricane Glass

Magic Flute
Scale ingredients to servings

2 oz Mozart® White chocolate liqueur
1 oz amaretto almond liqueur

Shake ingredients well in a shaker. Strain into a cocktail glass glass over three or four ice cubes, and serve.

Magic Star
3 parts white Creme de Cacao
2 parts Kiwi liqueur
3 parts Pisang Ambon
2 parts Cream
1 dash Grenadine

Preparation Instructions:
Shake all ingredients in a shaker until chilled. Gaurnish with chocolate power and a star made of fruit. Be creative.

Serve In:
cocktail glass

Mai Tai
- 1/2 oz. Curacao, orange
- 1 oz. Rum, dark
- 1 oz. Rum, light
- 1/3 oz. (fresh) Lime Juice
- 1/2 oz. Orgeat Syrup
- 1/6 oz. Sugar Syrup

Mixing Instructions

Shake everything except the dark rum in a shaker filled with ice. Strain into a highball glass over crushed ice. Float with the rum and garnish with a pineapple spear, lime peel and a straw.

Malibu Express
1 oz Malibu® coconut rum
1 oz light rum
2 oz 7-Up® soda
5 oz pineapple juice

Blend and serve on ice.

Malibu Twister
Ingredients:
2 parts Malibu rum
2 parts Tropicana (orange,straw.,pinapple)
1 part Cranberry juice

Mixing instructions:
Add rum & trister then, add cranberry jucie,stir

Manhattan Cocktail
Scale ingredients to servings

3/4 oz sweet vermouth
2 1/2 oz bourbon whiskey
1 dash Angostura® bitters
1 maraschino cherry
1 twist orange peel

Combine the vermouth, bourbon whiskey, and bitters with 2 - 3 ice cubes in a mixing glass. Stir gently, don't bruise the spirits and cloud the drink. Place the cherry in a chilled cocktail glass and strain the whiskey mixture over the cherry. Rub the cut edge of the orange peel over the rim of the glass and twist it over the drink to release the oils but don't drop it in.

VARIATION: No bitters. Substitute a twist of lime for the cherry and orange. Hold the lime twist in a lighted match over the drink and then drop it in. The heat really zips up the lime flavor.

Manhattan Iced Tea
Scale ingredients to servings

1 oz bourbon whiskey
1 oz Scotch whisky
1 oz tequila
1 oz brandy
2 oz sweet and sour mix
1 splash Coca-Cola®

Fill a collins with ice. Add and mix all ingredients. Garnish with a lemon, and serve.

Man o' War

Scale ingredients to servings

1 1/2 oz Wild Turkey® 101 bourbon whiskey
1 oz Orange Curacao liqueur
1/2 oz sweet vermouth
1/2 ozfresh orange juice

Shake all ingredients well with ice and pour on the rocks in an old-fashioned glass. Garnish with a slice of orange and a cherry, and serve.

Margarita Cocktail (Basic)

Scale ingredients to servings

1 1/2 oz tequila
1/2 ozpremium triple sec (preferably Cointreau)
1 oz lime juice

Rum the rim of a cocktail glass with lime juice, and dip in salt. Shake all ingredients with ice, strain into the glass, and serve.

Tip:
Wet the outside rim of the glass with a fresh lemon or lime wedge. When rimming with sugar or cocoa use one of the liquid ingredients to moisten the rim, preferably a flavored liqueur.

Matrix's Blue Pill recipe

Scale ingredients to servings

1 oz Patron® silver tequila
1 oz Bacardi® Limon rum
2 oz Alize® cognac or Hypnotq
1 splash 7-Up® soda

Add ice into the shaker and then, add the following liquors. Shake for 20 sec. Pour using a strainer into a low ball glass or a hurricane glass. Add a lemon slice for decoration.

Mekong
Scale ingredients to servings

1 1/2 oz Malibu® coconut rum
1/2 oz peach schnapps
1/2 oz strawberry schnapps
1/2 oz banana liqueur
1/2 - 3/4 oz melon liqueur
1/4 oz Blue Curacao liqueur
1/2 oz orange juice
1/2 oz pineapple juice
1/4 - 1/2 oz pina colada mix
1 dash 7-Up® soda
1 splash heavy cream

Mix the first ten ingredients (malibu, peach, strawberry, banana, melon, blue, orange juice, pineapple juice, pina mix, 7-up) in a shaker. Pour into a hurricane glass, then top with cream. Serve with fresh fruit (except lime), and some filberts if desired.

MELON BALL (Shot)
Ingredients:
•1/4 oz. melon liqueur
•1/4 oz. pineapple juice
•1/2 oz. vodka

Mixing instructions:
Strain into shot glass.

Mexican Firing

Lime juice, simple syrup, pomegranate molasses and white tequila shaken, not stirred. Blindfold me before I go down.

Serves: 1
2 ounces white tequila
1 ounce lime juice
1 ounce simple syrup
1 teaspoon pomegranate molasses
2 dashes Angostura bitters
1 lime peel, for garnish
1 lemon peel, for garnish
Add to favorites

1.Fill a shaker with ice. Pour in all of the ingredients, and shake until the outside of the shaker has frosted. Strain into a rocks glass over one large ice cube. Garnish with lime and lemon peel.
Optional:
Try substituting some jalapeno-infused tequila, or add a few slivers of fresh jalapeno to add more heat and complexity to the cocktail.

Miami Vice recipe

Scale ingredients to servings

5 oz Bacardi® 151 rum
1 packagefrozen pina colada mix
1 packagefrozen daiquiri mix

. . .

1. Mix pina colada with 2.5 oz. of rum w/ ice. Set aside.

2. Mix daiquiri with 2.5 oz. of rum w/ ice.

3. While frozen, add pina colada mix to a cocktail glass. Add the daiquiri mix on top, keeping it seperated from the pina colada mix. Serve.

Midori Colada
2 parts Midori Melon Liqueur
1 part White Rum
4 parts Pineapple Juice
2 parts Coconut Cream

Midori Colada Mixing Directions
 Blend ingredients. Best served in a hurricane glass with a straw.

Mind Eraser (Shot)
1/2 oz vodka
1/2 oz Midori melon liqueur
1/2 oz Bacardi 151 rum
1/2 oz lime juice

Directions
Shake with ice, strain into a shot glass and serve

Mint Julep
Bourbon 2 ½ oz
Fresh mint sprigs 6
Sugar syrup ½ oz
Orange slice 1
Lemon slice 1

Preparation:
Place 5 mint sprigs into a Collins glass and add the syrup, mixing to coat the mint. Add 1 ½ oz of bourbon and stir. Fill the glass

with ice and the remaining bourbon. Stir well and add the garnishes and remaining mint sprig.

Mojito
Ingredients

1 oz White Rum
1 oz Spearmint Schnapps
1 oz Triple Sec
1/3 lime juice

fill club soda ice rocks

Mojo
Scale ingredients to servings

1 qt light rum
1 qt dark rum
1 pint cherry brandy
6 cans light beer
5 cans 7-Up® soda
4 qt pineapple juice
2 bags ice

Mix all ingredients in a large container. Keep stirred.

Molotov Cocktail (Shot)
Molotov Cocktail Ingredients
∘1 splash Vodka

Molotov Cocktail Mixing Directions
 Pour a shot of vodka (preferably russian) into a shot glass. Float the 151, ignite, blow out, and shoot.

Serve In:

Shot Glass

Monkeys Ass
1/2 oz Bacardi 151 Rum
1/2 oz 99 Bananas Schnapps
3-5 drops Jagermeister

Preparation Instructions:
 Pour the 99 Bananas Schnapps in the shot glass first. Then add
the Bacardi 151 Rum on top. Add 3-5 drops of Jagermeister.

Additional/Optional Info:
 Best when chilled. Great group shot!!!!

Serve In: shot glass

Morning After
2 oz Seagram's® 7 whisky
2 oz DeKuyper® Hot Damn cinnamon schnapps
4 oz Captain Morgan® Original spiced rum
8 oz Mountain Dew® lime soda

Stir the whisky, schnapps and rum together in a large glass, Fill
with Mountain Dew lime soda, and serve.

N
Naked Barbie
1 oz Malibu® coconut rum
1/2 oz strawberry liqueur
5 oz pineapple juice

Pour all ingredients into glass over ice.

Naughty Nick

Scale ingredients to servings

2 oz McCormick's® vodka
5 oz Mountain Dew® citrus soda

Fill a glass with cubed ice. Add McCormick's vodka. Fill the rest of the glass with Mountain Dew. Stir and enjoy.

Nazi Cola

Scale ingredients to servings

1 oz Jagermeister® herbal liqueur
1 oz Rumple Minze® peppermint liqueur
 Coca-Cola®

Combine jagermeister and rumple minze over ice in a cocktail glass. Fill with cola, and serve.

911 (Shot)

Scale ingredients to servings

1/3 oz Goldschlager® cinnamon schnapps
1/3 oz Aftershock® Cool Citrus mint schnapps
1/3 oz Firewater® cinnamon schnapps

Add to a shot glass, and shoot.

Nipple On Fire

Scale ingredients to servings
1/3 oz butterscotch schnapps
1/3 oz Firewater® cinnamon schnapps
1/3 oz Irish cream

Pour in order into a shot glass; butterscotch, firewater, and float the irish cream.

NyQuil

3/4 oz Absolut® vodka
1/4 oz Jagermeister® herbal liqueur
 food coloring

Add vodka and jagermeister to a shot glass. Add a few drops of green food coloring, mix, and serve

O

Octopus

Scale ingredients to servings

1/3 oz Absolut® vodka
1/3 oz Rumple Minze® peppermint liqueur
1/3 oz Bacardi® 151 rum
8 drops Bailey's® Irish cream

Pour Absolut, Rumpleminze, and Bacardi 151 into a shot glass. Using a stir stick, drip in 8 drops of Bailey's Irish Cream one at a time to form the tentacles of the Octopus. Serve.

Oil Rig

 1 oz cheap Scotch whisky
1 oz peppermint schnapps

Pour both ingredients into a double shot glass (or whiskey sour glass, etc.) and serve.

Serve In: Sour Glass

OJ's Revenge

OJ's Revenge is more of a punch than anything; good to share with friends. For a better tasting version, use premium orange juice along with Jose Cuervo tequila, and Smirnoff Rasberry Twist Vodka.

Scale ingredients to servings

1/2 liter orange juice
1/2 liter tequila
2 oz raspberry vodka

Drink out of an orange juice carton until about 3/4 or 1/2 full. Fill the carton the rest of the way with tequila (almost to the top), then pour just a little raspberry vodka in. Put the top back on the carton and mix very well.

Stand in a circle with friends, take a swig of it, and then pass it around the circle until it's empty.

Old Fashioned

Scale ingredients to servings

2 oz bourbon whiskey
2 dashes Angostura® bitters
1 splash water
1 tsp sugar
1 maraschino cherry
1 orange wedge

Mix sugar, water and angostura bitters in an old-fashioned glass. Drop in a cherry and an orange wedge. Muddle into a paste using a muddler or the back end of a spoon. Pour in bourbon, fill with ice cubes, and stir.

Old Fashioned (Sweet) #2 recipe

1 oz brandy
1 tsp sugar
5 drops bitters
2 oz 7-Up® soda
1 splash grenadine syrup

Add drops of bitters to bottom of glass and stir in sugar. Once bitters and sugar are combined, add ice and pour in brandy. Top off with 7-up/Sprite and add a splash of grenadine. Serve with cherry/orange slice. Also works with whiskey.

Orange Bliss

Ingredients:
1 1/2 oz Orange vodka (Stoli)
1 oz Grand Marnier
3 1/2 oz Orange juice
Mixing instructions:
Shake with ice and strain into old-fashioned glass.

Optional: Cut a 1/4 inch slice of orange and place at the bottom of the glass before pouring.

Orange Rush

1 oz Bacardi® orange rum
1/2 oz peach schnapps
2 oz orange juice
1 oz pineapple juice
1 oz cranberry juice

Blend ingredients with ice. Serve in a tall glass and garnish with a slice of orange.

Orgasm

Scale ingredients to servings

1/2 oz white creme de cacao
1/2 oz amaretto almond liqueur
1/2 oz triple sec
1/2 oz vodka
1 oz light cream

Shake all ingredients with ice, strain into a chilled cocktail glass, and serve.

P
Pain Killer
Scale ingredients to servings

1 1/2 oz Midori® melon liqueur
 cranberry juice
 orange juice
 pineapple juice
1/2 oz Bacardi® 151 rum

Pour midori melon liqueur in an ice-filled collins glass. Almost-fill, with equal parts; cranberry, orange, and pineapple juice. Add rum, garnish with a cherry, and serve.

Paloma

For a refreshing, thirst quenching tequila cocktail, the Paloma is definitely at the top of the list and it's a favorite in Mexico. It's a light, fruity drink with a fizz and one of the smoothest tequila drinks out there. Almost any blanco tequila works well in combination with the grapefruit and you may also see this cocktail with grapefruit juice and a splash of soda instead of a grapefruit soda like Squirt.

Ingredients:
- 2 oz blanco or reposado tequila
- 6 oz fresh grapefruit soda
- 1/2 oz lime juice
- salt for rimming (optional)

Preparation:

1. Rim a collins glass with salt.
2. Fill the glass with ice and add the tequila and lime juice.
3. Top it off with grapefruit soda.

Paralyzer
1/2 oz tequila
1/2 oz vodka
1/2 oz Kahlua coffee liqueur
4 oz light cream
4 1/2 oz Coca-Cola

Directions
Pour tequilla, vodka and kahlua over ice in a collins glass. Half-fill with coke, and top with light cream or milk. Stir gently with a straw, and serve.

Pink Ranger (Shot)
1 oz vodka
1/2 oz coconut rum
1/2 oz Peach schnapps
1 splash cranberry juice

1/2 oz of Razzmatazz
1 splash of grenedine
1 splash pineapple juice

Preparation Instructions:
Mix all ingredients in a shaker, chill, and strain into a shot glass.

Pimp Cocktail
2 oz Absolute Vodka
1 oz Blue Curacao
1 oz peach schnapps
5 oz Sunny Delight orange juice
Pour ingrediants into a highball glass, stir and serve.

Pina Coleda
A casual drink that holds court over Hawaii

8 oz Pineapple juice.
8 oz Coconut cream
6 oz Rum
Cherry
Slice of pineapple, orange or lime

In a blender, grind ice while gradually adding the pineapple, coconut cream and rum. Alternatively, use shaved ice. The ice should be thick enough to hold a cherry on top without sinking in. Serve in a tall glass with a straw. Garnish with one cherry and a slice of fruit. Insert a paper umbrella for that additional tropical, exotic touch.

Prison Bitch
1 oz vodka
1/2 oz triple sec
1/2 oz amaretto almond liqueur
2 oz cranberry juice
2 oz orange juice

Shake ingredients in a cocktail shaker with ice. Pour into tall glass.

Punch in the Head
Scale ingredients to servings

1/3 oz light rum
1/3 oz melon liqueur
1/3 oz Southern Comfort® peach liqueur
1 oz cranberry juice
1 splash orange juice

Shake well and serve in a rocks glass.

Q

Quagmyre
Scale ingredients to servings

1/2 oz Canadian Club® whisky
1/2 oz Bailey's® Irish cream
2 oz chocolate milk
1 1/2 oz Kahlua® coffee liqueur
1 1/2 oz Perrier® soda water

Pour ingredients into a brandy snifter. Shake until clear, and serve.

Quaker's Cocktail
Scale ingredients to servings

3/4 oz light rum
3/4 oz brandy
 juice of 1/4 lemons
2 tsp raspberry syrup

Shake all ingredients with ice, strain into a cocktail glass, and serve.

Queen Soda
Scale ingredients to servings

2 oz butterscotch schnapps
 cream soda

Stir and serve in a highball glass with three or four ice cubes.

Quick Fox
Scale ingredients to servings

1 oz Irish cream
1 oz melon liqueur
1 oz Kahlua® coffee liqueur

Carefully layer each ingredient on top of the previous and serve.

Quickie
Scale ingredients to servings

1 oz bourbon whiskey
1 oz white rum
1/4 oz triple sec

Shake with ice and strain into a cocktail glass.

Quicksand

My wife loves" mudslides", but they are a little 'weak' for me.
Hence quicksand; a creation of my basement bar. Delicious,
with a little extra...almost undetectable...kick.
Scale ingredients to servings

1 oz Bacardi® Select rum
1 oz Bailey's® Irish cream
1 oz Kahlua® coffee liqueur
2 scoops vanilla ice cream (ie. Breyer's)
 handful ice cubes
1 dash(small glop) Hershey's® chocolate syrup
1 stick Kit Kat® chocolate bar

Blend all (very well) except the Kit Kat. After pouring into glass, add Kit Kat as a decorative stirrer before serving.

Quilt Lifter
Scale ingredients to servings

1 oz white rum
1/2 oz dry sherry
1/2 oz creme de bananes
1 oz pineapple juice
1 oz orange juice
1/2 oz passion-fruit juice

Shake briefly with a glassful of crushed ice in a double-cocktail glass. Garnish with fruit, and serve.

R
Raging Bull
2 1/2 cl Kahlua® coffee liqueur
2 1/2 cl sambuca
1 cl tequila

Layer in a shot glass; in order.

Raging Indian

1/4 shot Everclear® alcohol
1/4 shot Kahlua® coffee liqueur
1/4 shot orange juice
1/4 shot mango juice

Mix ingredients together in a shaker. Strain into a shot glass, and serve

Rain Man

Scale ingredients to servings

1 1/4 oz 151 proof rum
3/4 oz Midori® melon liqueur
4 oz orange juice

Shake all ingredients together, pour into a hurricane glass filled with ice, and serve.

Red Death

1/2 oz vodka
1/2 oz Southern Comfort® peach liqueur
1/2 oz amaretto almond liqueur
1/2 oz triple sec
1/2 oz sloe gin
1/2 oz lime juice
 orange juice

Pour all ingredients (except orange juice) into an ice-filled collins glass. Fill with orange juice, and serve.

Red Dog Recipe

1/2 oz Orange Vodka
2 oz Canadian Whiskey
1 1/2 oz Cranberry Juice
1 1/2 oz Orange Juice

3 oz Ginger Ale

Pour vodka and whiskey into a cocktail shaker. Add orange and cranberry juice, and shake vigorously. Pour over ice in a frozen or chilled collins glass or tumbler. Slowly add the ginger ale, garnish with a maraschino cherry or orange wedge, and serve.

Serve Red Dog in a Collins Glass

Red Eye
3/4 glass beer
1 oz vodka
 tomato juice

Preparation Instructions:
 Pour vodka into a beer glass one half to three-quarters filled with beer. Top with tomato juice, and serve in a beer mug.

Red Kiss
2 oz. Mandarin orange vodka
½ oz. simple syrup
Juice of one lemon
¼ oz. Chambord

Combine vodka, simple syrup and the lemon in a shaker filled with crushed ice (or ice). Shake and strain into a sugar rimmed glass. You will enjoy this sweet sensation bachelor party drink.

Red Headed Slut

1 ounce Cranberry Juice

1/2 ounce Peach Schnapps

3/4 ounce Jägermeister

Combine all ingredients in a cocktail shaker with ice. Shake to blend and chill. Strain into a large shot glass. Take this one fast for the sheer pleasure.

Is it the name, the taste or a little of both that get a rise out of the shot crowd? The Red Headed Slut goes for the mix of a cocktail, yet shoots straight for excitement.

RUM AND COLA JELLO SHOTS

Ingredients:
•6 oz. Jello
(1 box of CHERRY flavored jello) •2 cups Cola
(half in boiled mixture - half chilled for use later) •2 cups light rum

Mixing instructions:
In a bowl, pour the boiling water and 1 cup of cola over the Jello and stir until thoroughly dissolved. Cool to room temperature, then stir in 1 cup chilled cola and rum. Pour the mixture into shot glasses or Jello shot cups. Refrigerate until well-set, at least 6 hours. Makes approximately 32 1-ounce jello shots

Russian Banana

2 oz vodka
2 oz brown crème de cacao
2 oz banana liqueur
2 oz light cream

Shake with ice and strain into a highball glass.

Russian Iceberg

1 oz white creme de menthe
1 oz Rumple Minze peppermint liqueur
1 oz vodka

Preparation Instructions:
 Lean an ice-filled tumbler to a 45 degree angle and pour creme de menthe down the side of the glass to fill bottom. Repeat with rumple minze and vodka, as to layer the liquors like an iceberg. Do not stir. Place a straw through the middle of the drink and serve immediately.
Serve In:
old fashion glass

Rusty Nail
Serves: 1
Ice
2 ounces scotch
3/4 ounce (or so) Drambuie

1.Add ice to a short cocktail glass. Pour in scotch and Drambuie. Stir

S
Scooby Doo recipe
Don't forget to howl "Scooby-Doobie-Doooo..." before you drink.

Scale ingredients to servings

3 oz Everclear® alcohol
1 oz Bailey's® Irish cream
11 oz Coca-Cola®
1/2 oz milk

Pour all ingredients into a collins glass, and serve.

Screaming Chelsea

2 parts Vodka
2 parts Malibu
1/2 Orange juice (smooth)
4 Ice (crushed)
dash of Grenadine

Add the vodka and Malabu to a large glass, add the crushed ice.
fill the glass half way up with Orange juice (I used Tropicana)
mix the drink.
add a drizzle of grenadine down the middle of the glass.
the drink is in two colors.
now add lemonade until the glass is full enough.
give the drink another mix and the drink should now be bright
pink.

Screwdriver

Scale ingredients to servings

1.5 oz Smirnoff® No. 21 Vodka
6 ozorange juice

Add Smirnoff No.21 Vodka in ice-filled glass and top with
orange juice

747 Drink

The 747 Drink is made from vodka, Roses Lime, cranberry juice
and Sprite, and served in a highball glass.

- 1 shot Vodka
- Rose's Lime
- Cranberry Juice (white)
- 1 splash Lemon-Lime Soda
- Garnish: Lime Slice

747 Instructions:
- Fill a highball glass with ice.
- Add the vodka, and equal amounts of white cranberry juice and Roses Lime.
- Top with a splash of lemon-lime soda, and garnish with a lime slice

Sex on the Beach
- 2/3 oz. Schnapps, peach
- 1 1/3 oz. Vodka
- 1 1/3 oz. Cranberry Juice
- 1 1/3 oz. Orange Juice

Mixing Instructions:
Combine ingredients in a cocktail shaker with ice. Shake and strain into a highball glass filled with ice.

Shark
- 1 Tequila
- 1 Vodka
- 1 Tabasco

Mix and Serve

Singapore Sling
1 1/2 oz gin
1 oz pineapple juice
1 oz cherry brandy
1 tsp grenadine syrup
top with club soda

1 maraschino cherry
ice

Combine gin, cherry brandy, pineapple juice, and grenadine into a collins glass. Stir well. Top up with club soda and garnish with the cherry.

Serve in: Collins Glass

6-Shooter Recipe (Shot)
6-Shooter Ingredients
 °1/3 oz Kahlua coffee liqueur
 °1/3 oz butterscotch schnapps
 °1/3 oz amaretto almond liqueur
 °1/3 oz Jose Cuervo 1800 tequila
 °1/3 oz Goldschlager cinnamon schnapps
 °1/3 oz Bailey's Irish cream

6-Shooter Mixing Directions
 Stir ingredients together in a double-shot glass, and serve.

Serve In: Shot Glass

Sour Apple Kamikaze
1 oz Vodka
1 oz Sour Apple Schnapps
 fill sweet sour mix

ice (shake) rocks or up (use 1/2 amount of mixes for shots) Add 2 oz flavor mix or Schnapps for a Cherry, Peach, Blackberry, Raspberry, Strawberry, or Wildberry Sour Apple KamiKaze

Special K
1 oz Jack Daniel's® Tennessee whiskey
1 oz Southern Comfort® peach liqueur

fill with sweet and sour mix
1 splash orange juice
1 dash grenadine syrup

Mix all ingredients in a hurricane glass. Garnish with orange slice and a cherry.

Spicy Martini
Scale ingredients to servings

5 oz gin
1 oz vermouth
15 drops Tabasco® sauce

Shake the Gin and Vermouth with ice in a shaker. Pour into a large Martini glass. Pour the tabasco into the finished drink. Stir very lightly.

Spymaster
1 1/2 oz vodka
1/2 oz creme de bananes
1/2 oz lemon juice
1 egg white

Preparation Instructions:
 Pour vodka, banana liqueur, lemon juice and egg white into a cocktail shaker half-filled with ice cubes. Shake, strain into an old-fashioned or rocks glass almost filled with ice cubes, and serve.

Strawberry Daiquiri
2 oz White Rum
½ oz Orange Liqueur
6 red strawberries
1 oz Lime Juice
½ tsp Superfine Sugar

Blend all ingredients with 2 scoops of ice until smooth. Pour into a 16 oz. glass. Add a straw and garnish with strawberry.

Swedish fish

1 oz Black Haus blackberry schnapps
1 oz triple sec
top with cranberry juice

Preparation Instructions:
Combine the Blackhaus and Triple Sec. Add Cranberry Juice until it tastes like a swedish fish candy.

T
Tall Blonde
Scale ingredients to servings

1/2 oz gin
1/2 oz vodka
1/2 oz Southern Comfort® peach liqueur
1 oz peach schnapps
3 oz orange juice

Add all ingredients into shaker filled with ice. Shake well fill into chilled martini glass.

Tanker
Scale ingredients to servings

3/4 oz Grey Goose® vodka
12 ozcan Keystone® Light lager

Pour a full can of Keystone Light into a beer mug. Add Grey Goose vodka (or any vodka that you might have), and serve.

Teabomb
If you are the kind of person who likes to go all out with their drinks, you can also make your own tea. Earl gray is probably the best. Let the tea cool a little and poor cold jager on top. The cold and hot, one after the other makes for a fun change of pace from the norm. Now, even though you wasted all that time, this drink is best when slammed. Have fun.

1 part Jagermeister® herbal liqueur
1 part AriZona® iced tea

Pour the iced tea into a highball glass so that its half full. Then pour the Jagermeister down the side of the glass so that the drink doesn't mix too much. Chug away, the tea at the bottom is the perfect chaser, you won't feel a thing. Easy drink'n.

Telegraph
Scale ingredients to servings

1 1/2 oz RedRum® rum
3/4 oz Stolichnaya® vodka
 ginger ale

In a shaker with ice, combine rum and vodka. Shake well and strain into a highball glass filled almost to the top with ice. Top off with ginger ale and stir gently.

Texas Prairie Fire

This is a great shot to dote test the "pica" tolerance of any group of people. Who will be the Last one to reach for the glass of Ice Water? You, your best buddy or the cute girl across the table?

Scale ingredients to servings

3/4 oz tequila
 lime juice
3 - 5 squirts Tabasco® sauce

Pour 3/4 shot of Tequila in shot glass, top off with lime juice, splash in tabasco sauce, and shoot.

Texas Tea

2 oz tequila
2 oz rum
2 oz vodka
2 oz gin
2 oz bourbon whiskey
2 oz triple sec
2 oz sweet and sour mix
Coca-Cola®

Fill a 1 gallon pitcher with ice. Add all the ingredients except the coca-cola. Stir, then add the coca-cola and stir again. Pour into your favorite glass with ice and enjoy.

Tidal Wave

1/2 oz Tanqueray® gin
1/2 oz light rum
1/2 oz Smirnoff® vodka

1/2 oz peach schnapps
2 oz orange juice
2 oz pineapple juice
1 dash grenadine syrup
Bacardi® 151 rum

Pour gin, vodka, rum and peach schnapps over ice in a collins glass. Add orange and pineapple juices, a dash of grenadine, and float 151 rum on top. Garnish with a piece of fresh cut pineapple. *The wave will sweep you away.*

Tiger Jack
1/2 shot grenadine syrup
2 shots Jack Daniel's® Tennessee whiskey
1 shot triple sec
orange juice

Pour a measure (depending on sweetness required 1/2 to 1 shot is average) of grenadine into a tall, cool glass. In a cocktail shaker, add ice, 2 shots of Jack, 1 shot of Triple Sec then top up with enough orange juice to fill the glass. Give it a good shake and pour slowly into the glass.

Ten Pin Gin
1 1/4 oz Mandarine Napoleon
1 1/2 oz Gin
1 oz Dry Vermouth
1/2 oz Lime Juice

1 oz Sugar Syrup
1 tsp Egg White

Best served in a Cocktail Glass.

Directions
Shake and strain into a cocktail glass. Add a squeeze of a lime peel strip, and discard. Garnish with slices of orange and lime, and serve. More info on how to make a Ten Pin Gin

T.K.O.
1/3 oz tequila
1/3 oz ouzo anise liqueur
1/3 oz Kahlua® coffee liqueur

Just pour off the amount into a shot glass. Shoot and enjoy

Tokyo Tea
1/2 oz vodka
1/2 oz rum
1/2 oz gin
1/2 oz tequila
1/2 oz triple sec
1 oz Midori® melon liqueur

Combine all ingredients in a cocktail shaker. Shake, strain into a small highball glass filled with ice, and serve.

Tom and Jerry
Tom and Jerry is a classic winter cocktail and a must try for every explorer of the drink world. It's a sweet, frothy warm drink that is flavored by dark rum and, usually, Cognac (other brandy can be used as well). It's best with hot milk which makes the drink thicker than if hot water were used.

If you do not like the thought of drinking raw eggs you can use on of the artificial egg substitutes. They're not quite the same but do the trick.

Ingredients:
- 1 egg
- 1/2 oz simple syrup or 1 tsp powdered sugar
- 1 oz dark rum
- 1 oz Cognac or brandy
- hot milk or hot water
- grated nutmeg for garnish

Preparation:

1. Separate the egg white from the egg yolk and beat them separately.
2. Fold the beaten eggs together and place into an Irish coffee glass.
3. Add the sugar or simple syrup, dark rum and brandy.
4. Fill with hot milk or hot water.
5. Stir well.
6. Garnish with grated nutmeg.

TWISTER
Ingredients:
- 4 oz. Lemon-lime soda
- 2 oz. vodka
- Juice of 1/2 lime

Mixing instructions:
Pour vodka and juice of lime into a highball glass over ice. Fill with lemon-lime soda and stir gently.

U

Uncle Jack

2 oz Bacardi® gold rum
4 ozdiet Pepsi® Vanilla cola

Mix 1/3 glass Bacardi Gold Rum with 2/3 glass of diet Pepsi vanilla with ice.

Uncle Sam recipe

Scale ingredients to servings

1/3 oz Aftershock® Hot & Cool cinnamon schnapps
1/3 oz Avalanche® peppermint schnapps
1/3 oz Rumple Minze® peppermint liqueur

Pour, or layer the three (preferably chilled) liquors into a shot glass

Undertaker

Invented by a bartender at the Black Mallard Hotel in New York City on the east side. Due to the upscale locale, the management would not let him put the name "Undertaker" on the menu.

Tastes just like a chilled espresso, but with a serious kick. A few can knock you over. The alcoholic effect sneaks up on you after the initial caffiene buzz from the espresso.

Scale ingredients to servings

3 oz vanilla vodka
1 oz Kahlua® coffee liqueur
1 oz creme de cacao
1 ozchilled espresso

In a martini shaker over ice, add the Vanilla Vodka, Kahlua, and Creme de Cacao. Shake. Strain ice and pour into a chilled martini or cocktail glass. Stir in the chilled espresso and serve.

Upside-Down Martini
Scale ingredients to servings

2 1/2 oz French vermouth
1 oz gin

Stir together in a mixing glass filled with ice. Strain into a chilled cocktail glass, garnish with a twist of lemon peel, and serve.

V
Vampire's Kiss
2 oz vodka
1/2 oz dry gin
1/2 oz dry vermouth
1 tbsp tequila
1 pinch salt
2 oz tomato juice

Shake with ice, strain over ice in an old-fashioned glass, and serve.

Venus on the Rocks
1 oz amaretto almond liqueur
2 oz peach schnapps
3 oz club soda

Pour into an old-fashioned glass with five ice cubes. Garnish
with a twist of lime, and serve.

Vicious Sid

1 1/2 oz light rum
1/2 oz Southern Comfort® peach liqueur
1/2 oz triple sec
1 oz lemon juice
1 dash bitters

Combine all of the ingredients in a shaker half-filled with ice
cubes. Shake well, and strain into an old-fashioned glass almost
filled with ice cubes.

Virgin Pussy

1 oz watermelon schnapps
1 oz cinnamon schnapps
1 pinch sugar

Pour both watermelon and cinnamon schnapps into a shot
glass. Add sugar, and serve.

Vodka Fizz

2 oz Vodka
2 oz Half-and-half
2 oz Limeade concentrate
Ice
1 pinch Nutmeg

Directions
Blend all ingredients, save nutmeg. Pour into large white wine
glass and sprinkle nutmeg on top.

Vodka Martini Cocktail

3 ounces vodka
1 ounce dry vermouth
1 cup ice cubes
3 olives

Directions
1. Combine vodka and dry vermouth in a cocktail mixing glass. Fill with ice and stir until chilled. Strain into a chilled martini glass.
2. Garnish with three olives on a toothpick.

Note:
If you prefer, you can garnish your vodka martini with a lemon twist instead of olives.

VODKA SOUR

Ingredients:
- 3/4 oz. lemon juice
- 1 1/2 oz. vodka
- 1 tsp. sugar syrup
- Lemon slice
- Maraschino cherry

Mixing instructions:
Mix all ingredients, except lemon slice and maraschino cherry, with cracked ice in a shaker or blender. Strain into a chilled Whiskey Sour glass and garnish with lemon slice and cherry.

Voodoo Doll
1/2 oz vodka
1/2 oz Chambord® raspberry liqueur
 orange juice
 cranberry juice

Add vodka and chambord to a shaker. Add orange juice and cranberry juice until desired taste. Shake and serve with ice in a cocktail glass.

W

Walk the Plank Recipe
1 oz Captain Morgan Original spiced rum
1 oz Malibu coconut rum
1 oz RedRum rum
 fill with 7-Up soda
2 cherries

Preparation Instructions:
 Pour rum over ice. Fill with 7-Up. Stir. Garnish with cherries.

Warm Woolly Sheep
Scale ingredients to servings

1 shot Scotch whisky
1 1/2 shots Drambuie® Scotch whisky
 fill with warm milk

Mix scotch and drambuie, then top with warm milk.

Water Melon Cosmo
Ingredients
 2 cups cubed seeded watermelon
 1 (1.5 fluid ounce) jigger vodka (such as Skyy®)
4 cubes ice, or as needed
 1 dash lime juice (optional)

 Directions
1. Blend watermelon in a blender until smooth; strain through a fine mesh strainer and discard pulp. Pour strained watermelon juice, and vodka into a cocktail shaker filled with ice; strain into a glass. Squeeze lime juice into the cocktail.

Water Melon Shots
A MUST HAVE FOR ALL THOSE PARTYING EXPERIENCES

1 part vodka
1 part amaretto almond liqueur
1 part southern comfort peach liqueur

filled with orange juice/pineapple juice
1 dash grenadine syrup

shake well with ice and pour into shot glass

Best served in groups of 4's

Water Moccasin
Scale ingredients to servings

1 oz peach schnapps
1 oz Crown Royal® Canadian whisky
1 dash triple sec
1 oz sweet and sour mix

Added ice and ingredients in a shaker. Shake well until top becomes frosted. Then poor in a shooter glass. This will be best yet smoothes shot you'll ever taste.

What the Hell
1 oz Apricot Brandy
1 oz gin
1 dash Lemon juice
1 oz dry vermouth

Shake, strain into low ball glass.

White Russian
•2/3 oz. Kahlua
•1 2/3 oz. Vodka
•1 oz. Cream

Mixing Instructions

Pour coffee liqueur and vodka into an old fashioned glass filled with ice. Float the cream on top and stir slowly.

Whiskey Sour

1 lemon -- Juiced
1/2 teaspoon powdered sugar
2 ounces blended whiskey
cracked ice

Fill a mixing glass with cracked ice. Add lemon juice, whiskey, and sugar. Shake and strain into a sour glass filled with ice cubes. Garnish with a slice of orange and a cherry.

Whiskey Swizzle

2 oz blended whiskey
1 dash bitters
1 1/2 oz lime juice
1 tsp superfine sugar
3 oz club soda

Directions
Pour the whiskey, bitters, lime juice and sugar into a cocktail shaker half-filled with ice cubes. Almost fill a collins glass with crushed ice and stir until the glass is frosted. Shake the contents of the cocktail shaker, and strain into the collins glass. Add club soda, add a swizzle stick, and serve.

WINES

In recent years Wine has become an incredibly popular drink for bachelor parties. Here are some helpful hints while you are planning a bachelor party that discuss wine and what foods to serve with each type.

Today there are many varieties of wines grown all over the world. It is a personal preference which type or producer of wine you select! Don't let anyone convince you that more expensive wines are better. One can find great bargains everyday for under $10.

With all the choices you have to pick today, it really comes down to three types of wine: Red, White and Sparkling. Each wine is great but some wines go better with different kinds of foods. We will give you advice on what most people consider to be the "Rule" with wines and food. Just remember everybody's tastes are different, so what tastes great to one person, might not be as good to another. It is best if you can experiment a little and find the wines you think are best.

It is most often considered appropriate to serve Red Wines (Cabernet Sauvignon, Merlots, etc...) go with meats and game, other wines to consider with meats are Syrah/Shiraz and Pinot Noirs.

White wines usually are best with lighter foods including fish, foul, and vegetables dishes. These wines include Chardonnay, Riesling, Chenin Blanc, and other white wines. Each of these wines has different characteristics, and each one can be complimentary to the food you are having or just drinking on its own.

Some examples:

Spicy foods – Shiraz or Red Zinfandel (fruity and bold)
Red Meat – Cabernet Sauvignon or Merlots (full body wine)

Pork and Game – Pinot Noir (lighter red)
Shellfish – Riesling or Champagnes (Methode Champenoise) – (Light, dry wine)
Ocean and Fresh water fish – Chardonnay's and Semillons (heavier White)

X

X recipe (Shot)
3/4 oz amaretto almond liqueur
3/4 oz wildberry schnapps
1 splash sweet and sour mix
1 splash Coca-Cola®

Mix all ingredients in mixing glass and shake with ice. Strain into glass and shoot.

Serve in: Shot Glass

Xanthia Cocktail recipe
3/4 oz cherry brandy
3/4 oz gin
3/4 oz Yellow Chartreuse®

Stir all ingredients with ice, strain into a cocktail glass, and serve.

Serve in: Cocktail Glass

Xanthor's Pants recipe
2 oz Jameson® Irish whiskey or other scotch
2 oz Bailey's® Irish cream
4 oz coffee

Mix 1 part Scotch with 1 part Bailey's (approximately half of a US coffee mug). Rapidly top off with hot coffee to mix. Stir to combine, if necessary.

Serve in: Coffee Mug

Xaviera recipe
3/4 oz triple sec
3/4 oz Kahlua® coffee liqueur
1/2 oz amaretto almond liqueur
1 oz whipping cream

Shake briefly with a glassful of crushed ice in a double-cocktail glass. Garnish with a slice of orange and a cherry, add short straws, and serve.

Serve in: Cocktail Glass

Xeres Cocktail recipe
2 oz dry sherry
1 dash orange bitters

Stir ingredients with ice, strain into a cocktail glass, and serve.

Serve in: Cocktail Glass

XYZ Cocktail recipe
1 oz light rum
1/2 oz triple sec
1 tbsp lemon juice

Shake all ingredients with ice, strain into a cocktail glass, and serve.

Y

Y2K Shot
Scale ingredients to servings

1 part Kahlua® coffee liqueur
2 parts Yukon Jack® Canadian whisky

Serve in a chilled glass.

Yellowjacket
A non-alcoholic drink

2 oz pineapple juice
2 oz orange juice
1 1/2 oz lemon juice

Pour the ingredients into a cocktail shaker half-filled with ice cubes, and shake well. Strain into an old-fashioned glass almost filled with ice cubes, and serve.

Yellow Parrot recipe
Scale ingredients to servings

3/4 oz Yellow Chartreuse®
3/4 oz apricot brandy
1/4 oz anisette

Stir with ice in a mixing glass. Strain into chilled cocktail glass.

Yellow Peril

Scale ingredients to servings

1 oz Finlandia® lime vodka
1 oz Galliano® herbal liqueur
1 oz Bols® creme de bananes
1 oz Cointreau® orange liqueur

Pour all 4 ingredients into a brandy snifter and swirl. This is powerful stuff - named after English traffic wardens! After two you'll sleep like a dream.

Z

Zippper

1/2 oz tequila
1/4 oz Grand Marnier® orange liqueur
1/4 oz cream

Combine all ingredients in a shaker with ice and stir to chill. Strain into shot glass

Zima Blaster

Scale ingredients to servings

12 oz Zima
3 oz Chambord® raspberry liqueur

Fill glass with ice. Pour in Chambord, then fill with Zima. Mix and enjoy.

Zombie

This cocktail does have the potential to turn you into a zombie - just as the name implies and many Zombie drinkers can attest to. It debuted at Don the Beachcomber restaurant in Hollywood in 1934 and it is still perfect to enjoy for a relaxing happy hour, tropical summer drink or a haunting Halloween party cocktail.

Ingredients:
- 1 1/4 oz lemon juice
- 1 oz dark rum
- 3/4 oz orange juice
- 1/2 oz cherry brandy
- 1/2 oz light rum
- 1/2 oz high-proof dark rum
- 2 dashes grenadine

Preparation:

1. Pour the ingredients into a cocktail shaker with ice.
2. Shake well.
3. Strain into a highball glass with crushed ice.

Because of the high content of Rum, this drink can be lit.

SPECIALITY DRINKS AND CONCOCTIONS

Making Dandelion Wine

During the Era of Prohibition, many people made Dandelion Wine. Dandelions are in season during the spring and summer months, but they lend themselves deliciously to a beverage you can serve year-round. April and May are the best months to harvest dandelions for the purpose of wine making in the Northern hemisphere

.

Ingredients:

package (7 g) dried brewing yeast
1/4 cup (60 mL) warm water
2 quarts (230 g) whole dandelion flowers Using 2 quarts+ of just the petals can make for a less bitter wine.[2]

4 quarts water (3.785 L)
1 cup (240 mL) orange juice
3 tablespoons (45 g) fresh lemon juice
3 tablespoons (45 g) fresh lime juice
1/2 teaspoon (1.25 g) powdered ginger
3 tablespoons (18 g) coarsely chopped orange zest; avoid any white pith
1 tablespoon (6 g) coarsely chopped lemon zest; avoid any white pith
6 cups (1200 g) sugar

1) Wash and clean the blossoms well. Think of it as a fruit or vegetable; you don't want bugs or dirt in your food. Remove all green material.

2)   Soak flowers for two days.

3)   Place the blossoms in the four quarts of water, along with the lime, orange, and lemon juices.

4)   Boiling the blossoms. Stir in the ginger, cloves, orange peels, lemon peels, and sugar. Bring the mix to a boil for an hour. This creates the 'infusion' that will later become wine after fermentation.

5)   Strain the dandelion liquid. Strain through filter papers (coffee filters are recommended). Let the infusion cool down for a while.

6)   Stir the yeast in while the infusion is still warm, but below 100 degrees F.

7)   Cover it and leave it alone, let it stand overnight.

8)   Pour it into bottles, poke a few holes in a balloon and place over the tops of the bottles to create an airlock, to keep out unwanted wild yeasts, and store them in a dark place for at least three weeks so that it can ferment. At this point you now have wine!

9)   Rack the wine several times, optionally. Racking means waiting until the wine clears, then siphoning or pouring the liquid into another container, leaving the lees (sediment) at the bottom of the first container.)

10) Cork and store the bottles in a cool place. Allow the wine some time to age. Most recipes recommend waiting at least six months, preferably a year.

BANANA BEER

Banana beer is made from bananas, mixed with a cereal flour (often sorghum flour) and fermented to an orange, alcoholic beverage. It is sweet and slightly hazy with a shelf life of several days under correct storage conditions. There are many variations in how the beer is made. For instance, *Urwaga* banana beer in Kenya is made from bananas and sorghum or millet and *Lubisi* is made from bananas and sorghum.

Ripe bananas (*Musa* spp.) are selected. In the rainy season unripe bananas can be left to finish ripening laid on a hurdle over the fire where the cooking is done. During the dry season bananas can be ripened by making a pit in the ground, covering the sides of the pit with green banana leaves, packing the bananas in to the pit and then covering them with banana leaves and earth. On one side of the pit a little ditch should be dug for a fire so that warmth and smoke can enter the pit. This takes about six days. The bananas should then be peeled. If the peels cannot be removed by hand then the bananas are not sufficiently ripe.

The first step is the preparation of the banana juice. The extraction of a high yield of banana juice without excessive browning or contamination by spoilage micro-organisms and proper filtration to produce a clear product is of great importance. Grass can be used to squeeze the banana so that only a clear juice is obtained. The residue will remain in the grass.

One volume of water should be added to every three volumes of banana juice. This makes the total soluble solids low enough for the yeast to act. Cereals are ground and roasted and added to improve the colour and flavour of the final product. The mixture is placed in a container, which is covered in polythene to ferment for 18 to 24 hours. The raw materials are not sterilised by boiling and therefore provide an excellent substrate for microbial growth. It is essential that proper hygienic procedures are followed and that all equipment is thoroughly sterilised to prevent contaminating bacteria from competing with the yeast and producing acid instead of alcohol. This can be done by cleaning with boiling water or with chlorine solution. Care is necessary to wash the equipment free of residual chlorine, as this would interfere with the actions of the yeast. Strict personal hygiene is also essential. For many traditional fermented products, the microorganisms responsible for the fermentation are unknown to scientists. However, there has been research to identify the micro-organisms involved in banana beer production. The main micro-organism is *Saccharomyces cerevisiae* which is the same organism that is involved in the production of grape wine. However, many other microorganisms were identified. These varied according to the region of production. After fermentation the product is filtered through cotton cloth.

Flow diagram

Raw materials	Ripe bananas
Peel	Peel by hand
Remove residue	Use grass to knead or squeeze out the juice. The residue will remain in the grass.
Mix with **clean water**	The water: banana juice ratio should be 1:3
Mix with cereal flour	Mix with ground and roasted cereals to local taste. For sorghum the ratio should be 1:12
Ferment	In plastic container. Leave to ferment for 18 to 24 hours.

Filter	Through cotton cloth
Pack	In one-litre plastic bottles with cork stoppers or equivalent

Packaging is usually only required to keep the product for its relatively short shelf life. Clean glass or plastic bottles should be used. The product should be kept in a cool place away from direct sunlight.

Making Whiskey from Scratch
Instructions

Put the 10 lbs. of corn into a burlap bag and wet it down with warm water. Set it aside in a room that's warm and dark. Leave it there for 10 days.

Check the bag, and when you see corn sprouts emerging from that bag that are at least ¼ inches in length, continue to the next step.

Empty the corn from the sack into a tub of water and remove all of the sprouts and roots from the kernels by rubbing them. Keep only the corn, and throw it into the container you will use for fermenting the whiskey. You can buy fermenters at wine-making supply shops or online (see Resources below).

Mash the kernels until they're all cracked with a pole. Add 5 gallons of boiling water to the mash, and after it cools, add the yeast.

Seal the fermenter and install a vent that's water sealed.

Let the mixture stand for a week or 10 days, then pour the liquid through a pillowcase to remove any solids.

Making Stout Beer
Instructions:

1) Soak the barley in 6 cups of water. After 10 minutes, boil the water with the barley in it.

2) Take the grains out of the water when it begins to boil. Place them in an additional bowl so they can cool. The grain and pot used for boiling will be extremely hot. Use appropriate protection when handling these items.

3) Add extract and boiling hops into the boiling water. Boil for 1 hour.

4) Add moss after 45 minutes of boiling.

5) Add hops after boiling and soak for 15 minutes.

6) Cool the mixture and drain excess yeast and other ingredients. The remaining liquid after the draining process is your stout home brew.

Making Pear Wine

Ingredients:

•2 gallons good quality sweet apple cider
•9-10 pounds pears, sliced and/or chopped, seeds and stems removed
•1 packet wine yeast, (Lalvin EC1118 or EC1122 is what I recommend)
•about 3 gallons water

Things you'll need besides the ingredients

•A five-gallon bucket for primary fermentation
•An airlock
•Knife for cutting and slicing
•Tubing for racking the cider
•A second five-gallon container (bucket, carboy, jug, etc.) for secondary fermentation

Instructions for Making Apple Pear Cider

1.Make a yeast starter: Pour a little cider into a cup. Add the yeast. Set this out at room temperature. You'll know it's "working" when the mixture gets cloudy and foamy.
2.Wash the pears. Remove the stems. Cut up the pears, discarding brown spots, seeds, and any other parts that look a little questionable. Put the cut up pears in the bottom of your clean and sanitary primary fermentation container.
3.Boil about one gallon of water. Pour the boiling water over the into the bucket, on top of the pears. This is a form of flash-pastuerization, and should take care of any bacteria or wild yeast that might have been clinging to the fruit.
4.Into the bucket goes the sweet apple cider!
5.Stir the mixture.
6.Add the remaining water, about 2 gallons, until you have a total of five gallons of stuff in the bucket.

7.Allow the mixture to cool to room temperature. DO NOT add the yeast until the mixture is cool - high temperatures will kill your yeast!

8.When the mixture is room temperature, pitch the yeast starter into it. Give it a little stir.

9.If you are using a brewing bucket (like I have), put the lid on the bucket and affix an airlock. If you're using a regular bucket (nothing wrong with that!) simply cover the bucket with some tight plastic wrap. Make sure flies and other fruit-loving creatures can't get in.

10.Now you basically play the Waiting Game!

Primary Fermentation

Primary fermentation should take 1 to 2 weeks with this recipe. Regardless, I wouldn't leave the cider sitting with the fruit for much longer than that.

During this time, you'll see lots of activity in the airlock (if you're using one). The bubbles should slow down after about a week. At this point, you can rack the cider into a secondary fermentation container. This could be another bucket, a glass carboy, or a big bottle.

If you're using plastic wrap instead of a lid with an airlock, you'll probably notice the plastic wrap swelling during primary fermentation. This is the result of a buildup of carbon dioxide gas, a natural by-product of fermentation. You should remove the plastic wrap briefly every so often to allow the gas to escape. Again, after about one week, you will probably notice that there doesn't seem to be as much gas building up in the bucket. Time to rack the cider!

Racking:
Racking is a simple procedure in which a tube is used to siphon the liquid cider off of the sediments and other solids (including the pears).

To rack the cider using plastic tubing, place the bucket up on a table near the edge. Place the secondary fermentation container (whatever you've chosen to use) under the bucket, either on the floor or on a chair. Put one end of the tube down into the cider, but not all the way to the bottom of the bucket. In other words, try not to disturb the sediments with the tube. Suck on the other end of the tube until the cider flows, and get the tube into the secondary fermentation container quickly before you lose you're precious beverage - it comes out quick!

Alternatively, if you don't feel like using tubing for this first racking, you could just pour all of the liquid through cheese cloth to remove the solids. You'll want to rack the cider by siphoning eventually, at least when you bottle it, but for now it's not completely necessary.

Is five gallons a little more than you're looking for?

This recipe is for five gallons of apple-pear cider. It can be scaled down to as little as one gallon by dividing the ingredients. For instance, a one gallon batch of this stuff would call for 1/2 gallon of sweet cider, 1/2 gallon water, and 1 1/2 pounds of pears.

In general, try to include one gallon of water for every three pounds of pears used.

Secondary Fermentation and Aging

Secondary fermentation should take 1 to 3 months. This simply means that you will allow the cider to continue to ferment in the carboy or jug. This is usually a slower, less active fermentation, as most of the fruit sugars have already been used up.

The other purpose of secondary fermentation is to allow the cider to begin to clear - to allow the solid particles to fall out of suspension and collect on the bottom of the container, so that your final product will be more or less clear, rather than "soupy" looking.

So basically, wait around for 1 to 3 months, then rack the cider again. This time, you can separate the five-gallon batch into bottles if you'd like. I prefer 1-gallon bottles, as this makes my life simpler! Old wine bottles with clean and sanitary, and undamaged, corks work just fine. Jars with tight lids work well, too.

Aging:
The recommended aging period for cider is 6 months. This doesn't mean it won't be tasty three months after you started it! I'll wager that if you tried this recipe today, at the end of August, you'd be drinking delicious apple-pear cider in January.

But of course, the longer you allow the cider to age, the better it will be. That's part of why I like making larger batches - drink some, age some!

White House Honey Ale
The Official Ale of the White House — courtesy www.whitehouse.gov, Information Office

The White House Honey Brown Ale is the first alcohol brewed or distilled on the White House grounds. George Washington brewed beer and distilled whiskey at Mount Vernon and Thomas Jefferson made wine but there's no evidence that any beer has been brewed in the White House. (Although we do know there was some drinking during prohibition...)

White House Honey Ale
Ingredients

- 2 (3.3 lb) cans light malt extract
- 1 lb light dried malt extract
- 12 oz crushed amber crystal malt

- 8 oz Biscuit Malt
- 1 lb White House Honey
- 1 1/2 oz Kent Goldings Hop Pellets
- 1 1/2 oz Fuggles Hop pellets
- 2 tsp gypsum
- 1 pkg Windsor dry ale yeast
- 3/4 cup corn sugar for priming

Directions

1. In an 12 qt pot, steep the grains in a hop bag in 1 1/2 gallons of sterile water at 155 degrees for half an hour. Remove the grains.
2. Add the 2 cans of the malt extract and the dried extract and bring to a boil.
3. For the first flavoring, add the 1 1/2 oz Kent Goldings and 2 tsp of gypsum. Boil for 45 minutes.
4. For the second flavoring, add the 1/2 oz Fuggles hop pellets at the last minute of the boil.
5. Add the honey and boil for 5 more minutes.
6. Add 2 gallons chilled sterile water into the primary fermenter and add the hot wort into it. Top with more water to total 5 gallons. There is no need to strain.
7. Pitch yeast when wort temperature is between 70-80°. Fill airlock halfway with water.
8. Ferment at 68-72° for about seven days.
9. Rack to a secondary fermenter after five days and ferment for 14 more days.
10. To bottle, dissolve the corn sugar into 2 pints of boiling water for 15 minutes. Pour the mixture into an empty bottling bucket. Siphon the beer from the fermenter over it. Distribute priming sugar evenly. Siphon into bottles and cap. Let sit for 2 to 3 weeks at 75°.

DRINKING GAMES

1-2-3
1 dice
3 players

1. Each player rolls a die in turn.

2. The first to get a 6 names the drink. The second to get a 6 drinks it. The third, pays!

BASEBALL
4 shot glasses
1 quarter
4+ players

1. Set up the four shot glasses in a row going away from home base (the designated shooting spot for the quarter). Fill them with beer or similar beverage.

2. Each player on the visiting team takes turns shooting the quarter at the shot glasses. The first glass represents a single, the second a double, the third a triple, and the last a home run. Three strikes (misses of all shot glasses) and you are out. Three outs and the other team is up to bat.

3. The game follows as regular baseball and runs are scored in the same way (except that you have to keep track of the runners on base in your head).

4. If a player makes the quarter into a shot glass (gets a hit), he must drink the contents of the shot glasses behind the one he made. For example, if he hits a single, he must drink the remaining three shot glasses full of beer. If he hits a triple, he only has to drink one. If he gets an out, he must drink all four.

5. The opposite team must drink for each run the other team scores.

COPS AND ROBBERS

1 deck of cards
6+ players

Get a group of people (preferably at least 6 people) to sit around a table. Take a number of cards out of a deck that is equal to the number of people playing. One of the cards has to be a king and one of the cards has to be an ace. The other cards can be any combo of numbers people decide on. However, the higher the card number, the greater the chances of getting drunk quickly (you'll see why).

Pass out a card to each person.
Whoever receives the ace is the robber. Whoever receives the king is the cop.

2. Once all of the cards have been passed out, everyone stares at everyone else around the table waiting to hear the words "the deal has been made". These words will be heard once the person who has the ace (the robber) winks at someone.

3. The person who has the king (the cop) is on alert to try to see who the robber is. He/she wants to catch the robber winking at someone. Once "the deal has been made" (the person who is

winked at will say this to the group), the cop throws over his card and tries to guess who the robber is (the person who winked).

a) If the cop guesses wrong, he/she has to drink the number of drinks that the cardholder turns over.

b) This game, cops and robbers, continues on until the cop guesses who the robber is.

It's hilarious to watch the cop go through everyone around the table while having to slam beers for each wrong guess.

4. If the robber happens to wink at the cop, the robber is automatically busted and has to drink a pre-determined number of drinks.

DRUG DEALER

1 deck of cards
6+ players

Players should sit in a circle. Get as many cards as there are players for Drug Dealer. There should be one ace and one king mixed with the cards.

Any other cards will determine the the boot factor, so use lower value cards for less alcohol consumption, and vice-versa.

1. Mix up cards and distribute one to each player. Players look only at their own card. The player with the ace is the drug dealer and the person with the king is the cop.

2. The drug dealer must discreetly wink at any other player. Any player who sees the wink must then say "The deal has been made." The cop then identifies his/her self, and it is up to them to determine who the dealer is.

Note: If the cop sees the wink, the drug dealer must drink for 5 seconds. Play is restarted.

3. For each wrongly guessed player, the cop must drink the value on that players card. That card can then be removed.

4. When the cop guesses correctly, the drug dealer must drink the number of the remaining cards left between players.

5. The game is restarted once the drug dealer has been identified.

Drunk Driver

1 deck of cards

Pick as many cards as you have players. Pick one ace & one king and mix in the deck before you deal one card to each player. Players need to memorize their card. The player with the ace is the drug dealer and the player with the king is the cop.
The drug dealer must wink at the other players. Any player who sees the wink must then say "The deal is done." It is up to the cop to determine who the dealer is. For each wrong guess, the cop must drink for 10 seconds. Players may bluff and pretend they saw the wink even if they haven't which makes it a lot more fun.

This is fun with large groups of people because it is harder for the cop to guess. However, if the cop sees the wink, the dealer must drink for 10 seconds.

HOCKEY

1 deck of cards
4 players

1. Divide the players into teams of two. Partners sit across the table from each other, and the cards are all dealt out.

2. You score a point every time you lay the card of the same value as the person before you laid.

a) To make things more interesting, there are "safe cards": Eights and Jacks. You cannot lay a safe card on another safe card (i.e. no 8 on 8, J on J, 8 on J, J on 8).

3. The team that wins the point choses a player from the losing team to "knock". The other losing team player must drink until the other "knocks" for them.

4. After each point, record the point on a scoring tally. After all the cards have been laid, that's the end of a period (out of 3, as in hockey). The person to the left of the previous dealer becomes the new dealer.

5. Scoring:
a) Subtract the losing team's points from the winning team's points for each period. That will be the winning team's points for that period. (eg. Team A: 7pts, Team B: 5pts --- 7-5 = Team A: 2pts, Team B: 0pts)
b) Do the same for subsequent periods, and add the resultant scores for each period together for the winner.

KINGS

1 deck of cards
4+ players

1. Shuffle the cards. Start dealing one card at a time, face up, to each player.
2. The first person to be dealt a king picks a liquor, the second dealt a king picks the mixer, the third makes the drink (or buys it), and the last dealt a king drinks it.

Seconds

Seconds (named for the amount of seconds a person has to drink for in a given turn) is a card game. It uses a standard deck of playing cards. The play goes around the table with each player taking turns being either the "dealer" or the "drinker", with the former drawing the card that tells the latter how long to drink for. The drinker gets the chance to "challenge" the dealer which may lead to the opposite player doing the drinking.

Equipment:
1 Deck of Cards
2 or more people
Alcohol (most likely beer)

Origins:
The game was invented in Hopewell Valley, New Jersey in 2008 by college students Jon Bershad (me), Zach Nichols, and Takis Tzetzos while home on winter break from school. At a party, the three just started flipping cards and making the others drink based on the card's number. Eventually they began adding rules until Seconds was born.

Drunk Level:

Chances are the players will get pretty hammered, as the game consists mostly of just chugging for large amounts of time.

Official Rules:
The players sit in a circle with the shuffled deck of cards in the middle. Play goes around counter-clockwise with one person being the "dealer", and the person to his right being the "drinker".
The dealer picks a card. The drinker has to then drink for as many seconds (hence the name) as the number on the card. If the card is a face card, you just give it the corresponding number as its place in the deck (ie. Jack is 11 seconds, Queen is 12, King is 13, and Ace is 14).
Before the drinker drinks, however, he has a choice. He can take the number of that card, or he can challenge the dealer. If he challenges, the dealer draws another card.

*If the card is higher than the first card, the dealer has to drink the number on the higher card and the drinker doesn't have to drink anything.
*If, however, the second card is lower than the first, the drinker gets punished for challenging and getting it wrong and has to drink the combination of the two cards.
*On the rare instances that the drinker challenges and the second card is the same as the first, both the drinker and the dealer have to drink the combination of the two.

Once the seconds have been dealt out, the drinker becomes the new dealer and the person to his right becomes the new drinker and so on, around in a circle until you are out of cards or drink.

Optional Rule:
The game is occasionally played with the rule that if, at any time, the dealer draws a suicide king card (one of the two kings that appear to be stabbing themselves in the head), the drinker has to finish whatever drink they have in front of them.

THIRTY ONE

The game follows the same premise as Blackjack, but with some important variations.

1. The object of the game is to get as close to 31 points in your hand without going over. Aces are 11, all face cards are 10 points, and all other cards are face value.

2. Each player is dealt three cards, two face-down, and one face-up. The play rotates, like in Blackjack, for additional cards.

At any point in the game, if you think you have a high hand, 28 points or so, you can "knock," which means everyone else has one last draw to add to their hand. After everyone plays their last card, the hands are laid down.

a) The person with the lowest point total has to drink an entire beer before they lose again in an ensuing hand.

b) If the person who knocked has the lowest point total, that player must also drink an additional penalty beer for poor play.

c) If someone does not finish their beer before losing again, they must drink yet another penalty beer.

d) Finally, anytime someone has a total of 31 in their hand, they immediately place their cards down and everyone else is a loser (and must drink).

Three Man

Needed Tools: 1 Pair of Dice

Everyone starts off by rolling one die till someone rolls a three. That person then becomes the three man which is quite similar to the asshole. The game then proceeds around the circle with people taking turns rolling the dice. The dice are only passed when someone rolls something that does not require drinking. Here is what each roll means:

3: Whoever is the three man must drink. If the three man rolls this then he may pass the title to a person of his choosing.
7: Person to the right of "roller" drinks
9: Social... Everyone has a drink
10: Person to the right of "roller" drinks
11: Person to the left of "roller" drinks

Other dice combinations:

- 4 & 1: Whoeverrolls this gets to create a rule. There are many rules and you can have a lot ofun with it.

- Doubles: When someone rolls double they can give away drinks totaling the dice to any player or combination of players. One Exception: If you roll double sixes you have to drink 12!!

At any time during the game the three man can be told to drink.

UP AND DOWN THE RIVER
2 decks of cards
beer
6+ players

1. Everyone sits in a circle, one player is the dealer as well as a participant. Each player is dealt four cards face up, to be kept in front of that player.

2. The dealer then starts 'up the river' by turning over the first card.

a) Each player with the same card in front of him/her (suit doesn't matter), must take one drink.

b) If the person has more than one of the same card, it is a drink for each card.

3. The dealer then turns over the next card. Same thing, except this time it is two drinks. The next deal is three drinks, and the the last is four drinks.

4. After the fourth card, the dealer returns 'down the river' by dealing the next card on top of the fourth card dealt.

a) Players with matching cards now 'give' four drinks away in any combination; four to one player, or maybe one drink to four different players.

b) If the player has more than one of the same card; the player 'gives' drinks for each card.

5. The dealer continues back 'down the river' by dealing the next card on top of the third card dealt. This time players give three cards for each matching card. The next deal is a give of two drinks, and the last deal is a give of one drink.

6. After all the cards are dealt, simply shuffle and deal again. Lastly, the dealer starts turning over cards, while counting from 1 (ace) to 13 (king), if the count and the card turned over are equal in value then all players drink that many drinks.

7. Play continues until everyone is sick of the game, or sick from the beer.

FIXING HANGOVERS BLUES

Now you've done it and it's official, you have a hangover. Now what? No matter what you do sleep and water or juice should be included. There are many folk cures that are supposed to help cure a hangover. Many of them will help you cope by replenishing the vitamins and liquid you lost over night, while some like avoiding caffeine are very important to a quicker recovery. There is no one size fits all cure, find what works for you but the list below is a good place to start. There are also a few suggestions from readers who found their own way to cope.

Difficulty: Hard

Time Required: As long as it takes to feel better.

Here's How:
1.Sleep. Rest is your best friend at this point to give your body a recover. It is best to stay in bed so call in to work if you have to, tell them you have the stomach flu. You will sound so horrible on the phone they may believe you (unless they saw you at the bar, not a good idea then).
2.Replenish your body with fruit juice and water.
3.Avoid caffeine. A weak cup of coffee may be okay but a lot of caffeine will continue to dehydrate you, the opposite of what you want right now.
4.Drink orange juice for Vitamin C.
5.Drink a sports drink like Gatorade or Powerade.
6.Eat mineral rich food like pickles or canned fish.
7.In Poland, drinking pickle juice is a common remedy. Barbara Rolek, About.com Guide to Eastern European Food, has more Hangover Food suggestions from this region.
8.Drink a Bloody Mary. While the popular phrase "hair of the dog that bit you" may sound logical with a shot of whiskey left in the bottle next to your bed, it's only temporary. Try a Bloody Mary instead, while your blood is dealing with the new alcohol it is ignoring the old and in the meantime tomato juice and

celery are full of vitamins. If you drank the last of the vodka make a Virgin Mary. Another spicy morning after drink option is Hair of the Dog, in which gin and hot sauce are sure to bite your hangover back. Yet another classic option, sans spice, are the aptly named Corpse Reviver drinks: #1 (brandy), #2 (gin), #2011.

9.Take a shower, switching between cold and hot water.

10.In Ireland it was said that the cure for a hangover is to bury the ailing person up to the neck in moist river sand.

11.Try Alka Seltzer Morning Relief. One reader says that it's all that he and his wife have found that really works for them. He stumbled across this "cure" while his wife was still suffering after two days, within 15 minutes after taking the Alka Seltzer she was fine.

12.Get some exercise. Another reader suggests doing some sort of physical activity. He writes, "In the rare case of having hangover I usually drink about 1-2 liters of water and go outside to do some exercise like mountain climbing, swimming, cycling or just about anything that keeps me sweating." It takes willpower to move like that when standing seems like a challenge, but it is a good theory.

13.The side effects of aspirin, Tylenol and ibuprofen can be magnified when alcohol is in your system, so it is best (even though it may be the first thing you reach for) to avoid them to kill the hangover pain. Aspirin is a blood thinner, just like alcohol, and can intensify its effects and Tylenol (or acetaminophen) can cause more damage to your liver. Ibuprofen can also cause stomach bleeding. So be cautious when going for the quick relief.